IT'S
DEEPER
THAN
THAT

IT'S DEEPER THAN THAT

Pathway to a Vibrant,
Purposeful, and Liberated Life

SUZANNE ROBERTS

It's Deeper Than That: Pathway to a Vibrant, Purposeful, and Liberated Life
© 2025 Suzanne Roberts

Published by Thought Leader Academy Publishing
Thought Leader Academy Publishing
3901 N Kildare Ave
Chicago, Il 60641

Cover design by Claudine Mansour Design
Interior design by Liz Schreiter

Hardback ISBN: 978-1-968668-00-6
Paperback ISBN: 979-8-9922574-8-9
Audiobook ISBN: 978-1-968668-01-3
Ebook ISBN: 979-8-9922574-9-6

I dedicate this book to my mother,
Roslyn, and my brother Ralph.
I miss you both every day.

CONTENTS

"Listen to the reed flute,
how it tells of separation:
'Ever since they cut me from the reed bed,
I have made this crying sound.
Anyone apart from the source
longs to return to the time of union.'"

—*The Masnavi*, Rumi

PROLOGUE

*"If you want the truth, I'll tell you the truth
Listen to the secret sound, the real sound,
which is inside you."*

—Kabir

There is a treasure hidden inside of you, invisible to your eyes. This treasure may be unknown to you now, yet it is knowable within. It is the very essence of your being, a gift given from the source of life for all of creation Your deepest self resides inside of you, awaiting you. I am here to tell you that the gift of your life has already been given to you. You don't have to earn it or prove your worth—you get to awaken to that which is waiting for you inside of you.

Your *birthright* is your unapologetic radiance. This is what Polarity teaches.

Polarity is based on the laws of energy represented through a battery. It's an ideal operating energy system that provides guidance for your life purpose. This operating system resides within you. By discovering the wireless design, you'll access pathways and practices to guide you to your own inner radiance. With lifelong dedication, you have the opportunity to grow conscious of the truth of who you are. You can become a steward to the very essence of your own life.

———

This book is divided into three sections: Me, You, and Everyone. In Me, I share how Polarity saved me from suffering due to childhood trauma, returning me to my true life. In You, I teach you how to apply Polarity principles to guide you to your deepest, most vibrant, purposeful, and liberated self. In the final section of the book, Everyone, I show how life energy exists in all aspects of creation, including human-made systems, societies, and ideologies. By studying Polarity at this level, we learn that we're interconnected in the web of life.

Consider reading this book an invitation to take a walk. Yes, that's right—a walk. (As you'll see, being in nature is very important to me.) Walk alongside me on my journey from my deep knowing of interconnectedness at an early age to my slow disavowal of that knowledge by witnessing social disparities and harm in the world. Walk with me as I restore myself to my deepest knowing through Polarity. On this walk, I hope you'll discover, like I have, that personal and collective liberation are intricately intertwined. By applying the principles of Polarity, not only is it possible to reduce harm, it's also possible to become better human beings together.

———

I began studying Polarity Therapy when I was twenty years old, and I've been an ardent student and practitioner ever since. When I was first exploring Polarity Therapy, I was so curious about the inception of this methodology and body of work that I sought to learn more about its founder, Dr. Randolph Stone.

Stone was born in Austria on February 26, 1890. He emigrated to the United States in 1903 with his family. Stone studied Osteopathy, Naturopathy, and Chiropractic, earning degrees in all three areas. An avid lover of nature and the natural world, he preferred drugless and natural approaches to health and healing. During one of his many trips to India, he came across Ayurvedic Medicine. Having studied Chinese Medicine, Yoga, and Reflexology, Stone eventually synthesized his learnings and developed Polarity Therapy, an energetic approach to health and healing.

Stone's philosophy can be seen in this passage from one of his books, *Health Building*: "Health and happiness do not depend on the body, but on the energies that run it, flow through it and animate it. If we want health we must learn to govern and direct those energies from the center outward as a normal expression of life and motion, with a reverent attitude toward life's sacredness as the Creator's gift and we as its steward" (Stone 14). In just these few sentences, Stone's approach is abundantly clear: Health is a matter of sacredness and energy.

Stone became concerned that the allopathic medical system, or western medicine, was getting away from its symbol, the caduceus. The symbol of the caduceus consists of dual currents represented by snakes operating through a central core. Stone saw the medical world leaving this understanding behind with many advances in technology and specialization. He felt an urgent need for the medical world to remember the vital life energy as a resource for healing and health. Driven by this need, he authored a number of books: *Health Building*, *Polarity Therapy Volumes I and II*, and *Mystic Bible*.

Stone dedicated his life to serving his fellow human beings. While his practice was based in Chicago, he also traveled the world. Mysticism appealed to him, and he searched until he was eventually led to Science of the Soul. He became initiated into a meditation practice through Radha Soami Satsang Beas and dedicated himself to this practice the rest of his life. He eventually moved to India, where he spent the later years of his life, continuing to practice and serve people.

That's when I began studying Polarity Therapy, right after Stone moved to India. Though I didn't meet him, I heard many stories from his students and patients about his youthful spirit, joy of life, and dedication to life energy. I'm fortunate to have studied with students of his, to whom he passed the torch of Polarity Therapy. Polarity became an integral and foundational part of my life. My dedicated search and practice has taken me deeper and deeper inside of myself, bringing me greater equanimity, vibrancy, purpose, and liberation. I want this for each and every one of you.

Polarity has been central to my own life for fifty-two years. For much of that time, I've had the great fortune of running my own coaching and consulting company, UnifyingSolutions. Alongside my business, I taught Polarity. Now I'm bringing Polarity front and forward. After all, it's the deepest part of me.

I believe it will help you connect to the deepest part of yourself, too. That's why I wrote this book: I want everyone in the world that is hungry for deeper contact with themselves to have direct access to the power of life that is inside of them, underneath any personal or systemic trauma. Life existed before the hurt. Life energy will restore you to your wholeness and holiness within.

Note that the methodology in this book is referred to as *Polarity* rather than *Polarity Therapy*. Polarity Therapy consists of a therapeutic model with hands-on treatments, diet, and exercise. When I teach in person, I include hands-on techniques and relegate them to the nervous system and five elements; I aim to help people personally and collectively become vibrant and liberated. Engaging our parasympathetic nervous system supports our capacity for rest, stillness, pausing, and life-giving choices. And yet, while I have knowledge of all aspects of the Polarity Therapy model, what captivated my attention in Stone's writing was his "deeper than that," what he elucidated about our true purpose of life: soul consciousness operating through form to remember itself.

As a young student of Polarity Therapy, I spent eight years reading Volume I, combing through Stone's writing about everything from chemistry to psychology, underlining passages that stirred my longing. (That longing is what calls me, you, and everyone to greater depths of stillness and homecoming within.) In his writing, Stone poured out his inner knowing, his intellectual acumen, and life experiences—often in a random, disorganized manner. His books are hard to read yet contain gem after gem of wisdom. In *It's Deeper Than That*, I collect these gems, and create a simple, direct, and accessible approach to Polarity minus the therapeutic techniques and modalities.

Stone saw learning to control the mind as a critical part of becoming. As he writes in Book 3, under the section Limitations in Matter, "To learn to control our own mind is the real purpose of all experience, because the mind is the neuter agent of the very Essence of all matter in motion. All training, all experience, and even the suffering in life, have only one objective and that is to enable us to learn to control the mind substance within ourselves" (Stone 5). Yes. The mind rights the polarities so the soul can reign supreme. Then you truly return to who you are and have always been.

A quick note on how to read this book: Read the book straight through or go to individual sections that call to you. In the You section, there's a chart at the beginning of the first three chapters for you to refer to. You'll also find QR codes and links throughout the book to give you access to the book portal. Inside the portal you will find meditations to support you in your journey of inner stillness and accessing your inner radiance, and teaching videos for the first three chapters in the You section of the book. Throughout the book, there are questions to ponder which you will be able to access in the book portal as journaling prompts. Finally, you'll see the word "life" used in multiple ways. While most often, "life" is shorthand for life energy, at other times, it denotes life experiences. Context should make the usage clear.

I'm excited for you to enter into the world of Polarity. My life is forever changed, and I hope yours will be, too. I promise you: The "deeper than that" is inside of you, awaiting.

"Listen to your own Self. If you listen to that Self within, then you find the Truth."

—Kabir

PART I

ME:
MY JOURNEY FROM TRAUMA TO RESTORATION THROUGH POLARITY THERAPY

CHAPTER 1

IT'S DEEPER
THAN THAT

For as long as I could remember, my neck ached. When I was twenty, I set out to find a way to relieve myself of this great discomfort.

At nineteen, I had dropped out of The Ohio State University, where I'd studied pre-med, psychology, and modern dance. My mother was a doctor, and I was good at science; without a thought, I'd started on the pre-med track only to discover that I fainted at the sight of needles and blood. Once I came to terms with that, I had no idea what to do.

I did not want to study aimlessly, so I began searching for other ways of learning. I found a dancer's workshop in California with Anna Halprinn, a modern dancer who'd found healing through movement after her cancer diagnosis. Off to California I went! There, I pursued other areas of study by experts in their fields: I studied Jungian dream work, Gestalt Therapy, and Feldenkrais. I went to massage school and studied other modalities of health and healing. Along the way, I heard about Polarity Therapy from a friend.

At first, I was skeptical and curious. After all, I'd been raised with a medical framework that did not include any aspects of energy in its diagnosis or treatment, and Polarity Therapy is the study of energy in our body applied to health and healing. And yet what ultimately intrigued me was my love of physics and the laws of energy. I wondered how an energy-based system would approach health and healing.

And like that, I found myself climbing up the stairs to the second floor of a building in Berkeley. I walked in, and Jim Feil introduced himself to me.

Jim was a student of Dr. Randolph Stone, the founder of Polarity Therapy. Stone, a naturopath, osteopath, and chiropractor, had synthesized Ayurvedic, Chinese and traditional medicine and applied it to health and healing for the medicine world in his 1948 book *Energy*, where he first introduced Polarity Therapy. Fearful that the medical world was losing touch with the art of energy in the body, he was compelled to remind them, and the world, about this vital life force. I would learn all this later.

Since Polarity Therapy seemed to be about helping someone with their health, it made sense to me to ask Jim if he could help me with my neck. He looked at me with deep sincerity, kindness, and directness, and said, "It is much deeper than that."

I paused. This wasn't the answer I was expecting—or hoping for, for that matter—and yet it galvanized me to seek the greater depth inside myself since that day. My interest was finally piqued. My searching found a home.

In that class, Jim explained the fundamental principles of Polarity Therapy that reframed a way for me to find a vibrant, purposeful, and liberated life. He introduced a different framework about health and life based on a wireless system of energy living inside of me, you, and every human being. This system is designed to help us know ourselves at the deepest level within, the current of energy that gives us life and sustains us. In other words, there was a way to know something else besides what caused my neck pain.

Nothing else mattered to me at that point in my life. I began to live to study and know the "deeper than that" through Polarity Therapy. Polarity became the framework that reoriented me. It provided a pathway out of the despair, suffering, self-hatred, self-sacrifice, and shameful existence inside of me due to my trauma. I learned to treasure my life and myself and to value who I am. Polarity restored me.

CHAPTER 2

FROM TRAUMA
TO RESTORATION

Walking into my first Polarity Therapy class, I was not consciously thinking about my abuse. Even though my family members would sometimes remind me of my father raping me, I kept my memories tucked somewhere deep inside. I, like so many survivors, blocked my memories to be able to function in the world.

If it was not about my neck, what was it about?

My neck. Oh my neck. My neck. My neck. That was the start of wanting to die.

I was five, taking a bath at dusk. It had been a day of bike riding until sweat dripped down my back while my heart pounded, a day of climbing trees, of building teacups in the mud, and I needed to scrub the day's residue off of me. I remember having fun in that bath, thinking about my many adventures. Then I heard my dad come home.

I worshiped my dad. Many young girls see their dads as superheroes. (Maybe he trained me to worship him.) I just know that I flew out of the bath excited to see him. I dashed down the stairs with the anticipation of a little girl wanting what any child would want—her father to be overjoyed to see his daughter, to scoop her up in his arms. I was his only girl after three boys. Thrilled, I ran to him.

My dad did not return that enthusiasm by scooping me into his arms with delight or tenderness. His thrill was not about me. Instead, he was driven by his sexual urges and perversions. He made me captive. I saw a vacancy in his eyes, and I felt a cold chill run through me. I was his object of desire and prey, not a precious daughter. I was not real to him—I couldn't be—I never would be.

In that moment, I realized that what I wanted would not happen and what he wanted would. In a split second, I lost my innocence, my consent, my voice, my belief that my dad loved me, the safety of my heart in my body, and the safety of my body. Deflated and betrayed, my first kiss came as a rape. I was five years old. (I hate it when people ask, "When was your first kiss?")

He grabbed me and thrust me down on my back, right there on the living room floor. Then the unbelievable began to happen: I felt him pounding on me, into me.

I was feisty. Spirited. At first, I kicked and screamed, called for the police, desperate for my family members to come to my rescue. I fought hard. At that moment, I wanted to fight for my life. Because there were people in the house, my mom and my brothers, I thought my fighting might have a chance. Surely, someone would come to my rescue and join me in my vigorous flailing and anger.

My screaming did work. People did come—I saw them. Only they did not come to save me though. I saw them watching him rape me. When I saw that they were not going to help me in my fight, I wanted to die. Dying seemed so much better than lying there with my dad, heartless and cruel, penetrating me over and over again. Yes, I wanted to die, lying there with my family watching, frozen. I wanted their help, I wanted him off of me, and I wanted the nightmare I was living to stop.

I wanted my fight to matter.

My five-year-old body stood no chance against his stature and force. I started banging my head repeatedly to my right side (my family was to my left) with the hope that I could use my fight to at least knock myself out. I don't think I actually knocked myself out, but it provided an active distraction, a place to put my fight. This took me to a place that saved my life, a place guarded by my superheroes, my heroines: Grace, Mercy, and Love.

There, everything went quiet. In this sacred place, I felt held by Grace, Mercy, and Love, blanketed in pure compassion and eternal warmth. Here was a sense of spiritual knowing, of coming home to a true reality not of this world. Here was certainty. The physical world lost its value. No longer a safe place, it was unlivable at that moment. My heroines Grace, Mercy, and Love saved me.

So this is where the pain in my neck began. And what happened next contributed to the heinous experience.

Somehow, after the rape, I got dressed and ended up at our round dining room table. The six of us were there: me, my three brothers, our mom, our dad. I'm sure we had the usual plate of food: some kind of meat, a vegetable, a starch—maybe potatoes or rice. I don't remember eating. I have no recollection of exactly what was spoken, but people were talking. Talking to each other and ignoring me. I was so silent and in a complete state of shock that I did not contribute to the conversation. All I wanted to do was disappear.

At the same time, I wanted so badly for a member of my family to acknowledge my presence. What if one of them, just one of them, asked me how I was or addressed what had just happened? What if just one of them extended to me the help I needed? That's what deepened the hurt—how they erased the experience and me.

The neurological ability to not blame oneself develops around the age of ten. As a five-year-old, the only way I could understand what happened was by telling myself that I must be a horrible person to not only have this happen but for everyone to act like nothing was wrong. If everyone acted that way, maybe nothing was wrong. Maybe I was wrong. I wanted to die right then and there again. The pain, terror, and shame were overwhelming. I felt a terrible burning in my neck from repeatedly hitting my head against the floor. That ache formed the backdrop of my retreat deep inside myself. With pain as my companion, I would disappear. I would hide.

And yet again I found warmth and peace that enabled me to endure this unendurable moment. I clung to this internal mystery; I am certain it saved my life.

The abuse went on for another six years. I had many years of being sexually assaulted to practice wanting to die, hating myself, seeing myself as unworthy. I went on to hate myself for many, many years. I got trained to sacrifice myself and not trust my own experience. Now I know it was insanity that the people around me made me deny my experience and not even try to understand it. All of this would haunt me for years to come.

Jim was right. It was much deeper than my neck.

CHAPTER 3

FINDING
THE DEEPER

What did Jim mean by "deeper than that?" If it wasn't about my neck, what was it about? I began to listen as Jim introduced a different framework about health and life. This framework is based on a wireless system of energy living inside of me, you, and every human being. He explained the design of this wireless system is based on an energy current running inside our body. Here's how he broke it down:

- There is a primal source that is the supplier for this flow of energy.
- This energy is intelligent.
- We are sustained by this source and this energy flow.
- The whole of creation exists because of the source.
- This gift of this energy is the center of life within us, our own soul.

Source → Supply → Energy Flow. Wow! This was physics, my favorite subject in school. Physics gave me a way to make sense of the world when life at home did not.

When I was eleven, my father finally left. His absence did not immediately remake our home. In his shadow, the house was still chaotic. Some of my brothers exhibited violence towards one another. My mother was devastated—demoralized and depressed, sometimes suicidal. Somehow, I held it together to support my mom. I wanted to be invisible to my family's explosive anger; I worked to keep the violence from being directed at me. At the same time, I was still suppressing the trauma of abuse from my dad, trying to act normal, but it was exhausting. Focusing on school was hard. I had to act like I was okay.

I was not okay.

Physics class captured my attention. It made me feel alive. This was a reprieve from wanting to die and hating myself. Studying levers, mechanics, formulas, energy, motion, and how our world works reminded me that some things in life are measurable. Definable.

Back in Jim's class, I heard the echo of physics when he spoke of energy, motion, and movement. Polarity. I thought about how we switch on the lights in our home, and most of us are oblivious to the source of energy generating the electrical current. The supplier of that energy might be natural gas, coal, solar, wind, nuclear, oil, or biomass. What supplied *my* living energy? How was I animated by my primal source?

Physics had taught me to understand energy, resistance, current and flow in the outside world, but Jim's explanation of the wireless system gave me a way to understand physics inside of me. I discovered a longing inside of me, a longing to explore a way to know myself in relation to the source and this vital energy—instead of being defined by my trauma.

As Jim discussed the wireless system, my mind briefly stopped racing. Everything became still. When I'd been given the gift of life, why did I hate myself so much? If I was connected to a source for all of creation, how could I integrate this understanding into myself?

Posing these questions to myself was nothing short of a revelation. I could know myself as a radiant soul. Not the object of my father's cruelty. Not a worthless piece of shit. A radiant soul. My world shook.

I was enchanted. I was confused. I was challenged. Above all, I was hungry to know more. I recognized a scientific basis for understanding my life.

Impelled by this curiosity, my concerns about my neck faded into the background, and I was left with the "deeper than that" that Jim referred to. I knew I had a ways to go to accept this scientific reality as a way to truly know myself.

I recalled a similar feeling when I was four or five years old. I remembered playing outside in the summer as the sun began to set. I looked up at the sky and did not see an end. I thought the sky must go on forever and ever and ever. An awe awakened in me, the astonishment of being connected to the infinite. That wonder stirred in me when I found my heroines of Grace, Mercy, and Love during the darkest hours of my trauma. That feeling of amazement paralleled my wonder.

The eternal must live inside me. Science says so. In that moment, I wove together science, awe of the infinite, and my awareness of source through my heroines, Grace, Mercy, and Love. I desperately clung to this newfound framework. Polarity became my lifeline.

CHAPTER 4

INNER AND OUTER
LABORATORY

A few months later, I took my next Polarity class with Cindy
Brown Rawlinson. In her teaching, Cindy addressed the
deeper meaning and roots of the Polarity principles. After reading Dr. Stone's writings, we reflected on key passages to build
understanding of the material and connect to our inner knowing. Then we applied the understanding we'd cultivated to the
hands-on treatment for that day. Any technique we practiced
was coupled with the refrain, "It's deeper than that."

I'd studied pre-med; I was familiar with science laboratories.
Test tubes, chemical reactions, microscopes, slides: These I knew
how to engage with and operate. Now I wanted to find a way to
explore the unseen energy inside me. It was time to conduct my
own research, to validate the theory of Polarity I was studying. I
understood it intellectually, but I needed to know it for sure—in
other words, I needed to know it deeper than that.

I thought about how a battery operates. There needs to be
a liquid medium for the current to flow. In the body, the soul
pulses through the liquid medium of our cerebral spinal fluid. I'd

heard about cranial sacral methodology, where a practitioner can track the tides of the energy current, the soul current, through sensitive touch. This revelation made sense to me. The liquid medium in my body, my cerebral spinal fluid, conducts the energy of my soul just like a battery conducts energy.

I decided to explore in the laboratory of my body. I did this by bringing my attention inward toward my spine and imagining the pulsing of my soul inside of me. In this way, I could investigate the vibrant current of energy fluctuating inside of me. It wasn't easy. Such exploration required me to slow down, allowing myself to become aware of something elusive and etheric yet very real. The enormity of this experiment dawned on me. It would take a lot of practice, determination, and dedication to truly discover and know the power of this energy.

I began to devour Dr. Stone's writings in my free time. While they have a reputation for being opaque and disorganized—just plain difficult—I found them thrumming with vitality. Stone wrote in a stream-of-consciousness, unedited style, and this conveyed an inner knowing, the product of introspective research and science. Stone's writings are pulsing transmissions of knowledge. In them, he states that skill rests in understanding. As I read, I established the foundation of understanding that I would build upon for the rest of my life.

To seek the being of my soul, I needed to provide myself with experiences that allowed me to explore in the laboratory of my body. Being in nature became primary for me. There, I could find harmony and aliveness. I could feel myself more, un-numbing from the horror of my trauma. I lived surrounded by California redwoods, amidst beautiful hill country. I spent a lot of time hiking alone in dense forest, trekking to the ocean, and plunging into the frigid Pacific. The plunges helped me thaw from the impact of my traumas and regulate my nervous system.

Some friends of mine had an A-frame house in the woods in a small town, Nicasio. Behind it, on the property, was an old logger's cabin. One day, on a whim, they offered it to me. It needed to be rebuilt in order to make it livable.

I'd always wanted to build my own house, to live off the land—ideals shared by many young people at the time. So I agreed. It wasn't the one-person job I'd imagined, but a series of projects completed with friends. Though the work was arduous, I had my own home by the end of it. I installed a skylight. A wood-burning stove. Most importantly, I had nature, right there, safe, reassuring, invigorating. I would hike in the woods surrounding my cabin, and soon I found a fire road on a vast cow ranch. There I took refuge. I'd hike barefoot, climbing, breathing hard, smelling the eucalyptus trees, feeling the dirt and tiny rocks beneath my feet. I was glad to feel the dirt and rocks. I connected to the earth and awakened to my life. The breeze rustled through me.

Lying on my blanket, slowing down, I could feel a pulsing inside me, reciprocal with the earth and within me. I would lie there for hours just to deepen into my own battery, my own livingness, my own life. Once a month, I'd bring a sleeping bag and water to my place of refuge and spend the night. I would bring my handouts from Polarity class and Dr. Stone's notes, reflecting on them as I quieted into greater stillness.

It was there on the hillside, even though I was alone, that I felt the least alone that I'd perhaps ever felt. Laying on the earth, I felt a harmony with the heartbeat of life, where in all the diversity in nature, there was no sense of separation. In the quiet, I could hear the symphony of life inside me, not with my physical ears, but with my unselfconscious aliveness, like the waves of the ocean. When Dr. Stone wrote that it is our birthright and natural heritage to know our own soul, I connected to my heroines. They'd been with me all along—Grace, Mercy, and Love. That gave me the most hope.

There was something to inherit, an allotted part and parcel of the source, my soul, right inside of me. I began to realize that I was not going to be able to get rid of the voices of self-hatred and wanting to die overnight. I was going to have to dedicate myself to applying my attention to this path—to making the purpose of my life have a meaning that made sense to me. I needed to accept that I had the capacity. To believe that one day the voices would quiet. That my experience of aliveness and stillness at the depth of me would increase.

That's exactly what happened.

Fifty-two years later, my history of trauma is so faint. It's a broken bone that has healed. If you kick that spot, it hurts, but most of the time, it's not kicked. Today, I live vibrantly, with great purpose, liberated, whole, and holy. I am in tune with the being inside my body and grateful beyond words. It has been a long road, worthy of the trek.

CHAPTER 5

GROUNDED HOPE

Cindy Brown Rawlinson's teaching of Polarity profoundly influenced me in my next phase of learning. The slow pace provided time for self-reflection and a deepening understanding of the roadmaps and diagrams for the wireless system of energy. The emphasis on the living system gave me time to know how it lives inside of me. I began to realize that on some level, I already had knowledge of this, and now I was getting to know it consciously.

I was taught to pause, listen, and allow space for what is deep inside of me to guide me. This was contrary to how I was socialized to lead my life. This practice asked me to consider myself, which was not familiar to me at the time. I began working on quieting my mind by having a meditation practice. I walked in nature to be quiet and seek an inner listening. I aimed to sense the living energy inside of me for guidance. This required intentional practice, which set a foundation for the rest of my life. I began to lean on inner guidance.

And yet my newfound hope competed with my desire to die and my self-hatred. Somewhere inside of me, I wanted to live, but I didn't yet know how.

I ached to associate with the energy system of livingness, my own soulfulness. I wanted to be part of a bigger system like those I found in nature. I wanted more than to be defined by my trauma, but just because I longed for this transformation didn't mean it would happen quickly. After all, I'd built a life around surviving, getting through day after day. My mind created a story about me being bad. Deserving the abuse. Being unlovable. Unholy.

Looking back, I realize this was a brilliant survival tactic. While I was being abused, hating myself and wanting to die served as distractions. They took my mind off what was happening and helped me make sense, albeit imperfect sense, of horrific experiences to help me survive. My dear mind was only trying to help me.

As I realized my mind's ingenuity, I accepted it as a part of me. Soon, I needed to move from surviving to thriving. Yes. Radiance is the currency of life.

———

How could I trust this wireless system operating inside of me? How could I believe that what I was learning about was real and true?

In those days, *trust* wasn't part of my vocabulary. I didn't trust most people. I didn't even trust the world. The world seemed out of sync with what I knew about holiness. How would I learn to trust my own life?

There was one aspect of existence that I did trust: the place I went to for survival and the figures I found there. I trusted my heroines, Grace, Mercy, and Love. And Holiness. Holiness, I saw, was among the heroines, too. My heroines would be available whenever I sought them—I knew that. Whenever I summoned them, they offered me refuge. They never denied me access or hid themselves. The refuge I found became a sanctuary where no one could reach me. This is how I survived. I built a muscle of trust and instinctively began to use it for myself until I could live with conscious awareness of my holiness, which eventually gave me agency.

When my dad was raping me, I fought. Somewhere inside, I had the instinct to fight for myself. It's not surprising that I lost conscious touch with that part. I packed my instinct to fight into a dark, private space. Instead, I tracked the loss, defeat, help-lessness, hopelessness, and despair. My bold, powerful battle cry became a whisper I could no longer hear.

Yet my innate fight to live began working on my behalf in spite of my efforts to ignore it. The unconscious hunger to know the mystery within me propelled me to seek internally and exter-nally. I longed to know my own soul vibrancy, my link to the eternal unknown.

By studying Polarity Therapy, I learned that the wireless operating system worked within me whether I was a fighter or not. The internal design worked on my own behalf, with or without me. The soul operates through form to remember itself. Simple. Sensible. Direct.

Still, my existence defined by self-hatred was separate from my valiant inner warrior. They operated independently of each other, and there was a large gap between these realities. No bridge existed yet.

What helped build the bridge was applying my learning from Polarity in a practical, dedicated way. Every day after studying the wireless system, I'd look in the mirror and repeat to myself, "The source of life for all eternity has given me the gift of my life. My soul is radiant and pure." At first, I did not believe it, but truth wins out in the end.

I clung to rewiring my mind because I wanted to truly live. I wanted to feel more and more alive. I wanted to continue to live from affirming my value within. I wanted to find a way to help people transform trauma into a vibrant life. I wanted people to know their true value within. Over time, I came to celebrate and honor my own soul, my own life. I became more vibrant, more purposeful, and more liberated every day.

CHAPTER 6

APPLICATION OF MY LEARNING

My next Polarity Intensive took place in the Bay Area on Mt. Tamalpais at the Ralston White Retreat Center for six weeks. I studied with Jim Feil, Cindy Brown Rawlinson, and Ray Castellino. People from all over the country attended.

I don't think anyone knew how much I was suffering inside. On the outside, I was an engaging, friendly, and curious learner. But like other survivors suffering in silence, I lived in a dark corridor where only I knew the way in. In the darkness was an abscess unreachable by air or light. Polarity was teaching me that in spite of this suffering, there was the possibility for something more—a way to bring light and air to the darkness.

Those six weeks on Mt. Tamalpais, we lived Polarity. We followed Dr. Stone's cleansing and building diet from his book *Health Building*. The cleansing diet incorporates a liver flush concoction followed by tea in the morning and raw foods for lunch and dinner—sometimes a baked potato. The building diet follows the cleansing diet by adding in grains, beans, nuts, and small quantities of dairy. Dr. Stone was a vegetarian; all of his nutritional guidance is vegetarian.

We worked on self-dialoguing, training ourselves to observe the mental patterns of our mind. We'd sit in a chair and name out loud the mental patterns that were plaguing us. Then we'd move to another chair and respond to ourselves with the tenets of Polarity Principles. This required bringing forth neutrality, compassion, and understanding. We'd repeat this version of musical chairs until the mind softened its tenacious habit of repetitive thoughts. Repetitive thoughts, I was learning, are based on history or the future, never the present.

As I watched other people practice this technique, I gathered the courage to apply it to myself. I applied it my rape. If no one was raping me in the moment and therefore no one was watching me be raped, why was I continuing the banter of self-hatred? The groove of self-hatred was well etched, just like a needle getting stuck on a record. I could not get the needle off.

Slowly, I began to create another groove in my mind, a life-giving groove, one that reflected the truth about my soul vitality. I was learning about this system of wireless energy, whole unto itself, connected to a source, intelligent, and purposeful. If this system was connected to source, if it was whole unto itself, source energy must be inside me. If that were true, something was using me as a conduit, sending me love, grace and benevolence.

What I thought was the shit show of life was happening outside of me.

Through Polarity, I gained momentum in understanding that my soul vitality was my true life. Life was *inside* of me.

Slowly, I reframed my conception of life.

Every day, I stood in front of the mirror and repeated that the source of life had chosen me and given me the gift of life. It chose to reveal to me a way to survive that gave me a taste of its magnificence and refulgence. If that spark of energy and current was inside of me, maybe trauma didn't define me. Maybe I could find a way to belong and to matter to this precious life energy and this current instead of to my family. Maybe I could find a way to be at home inside myself. That's all I could think of. I held on with everything I could, repeating this over and over again.

Not that I believed it yet. I didn't. But I needed to orient my attention, or I'd be lost. I've since learned that Dr. Stone would say that you can't let go of something until you have something more life-giving to attach yourself to. I attached hard.

The more firmly I attached, the more I sensed an increase in the power of energy movement deep within the hands-on techniques. I felt engaged, awakened, fascinated. Being a witness to the power of energy movement within myself or another person brought me to a state of awe. That awe of holiness would bring me to my knees over and over again. Observing and sensing the soul vitality became fuel to fight for my own life. It is within me; it is within you; it is within everyone.

Any bodywork techniques we learned became tools to support a deeper purpose, greater contact with the vibrancy within, and more access to our own life forces. We did not approach the bodywork with an attitude of trying to fix someone or something. Instead, we learned to trust the inherent power of the wireless operating system. As a drop of the source for all life, the soul is intelligent.

And the wireless system has a purposeful and intelligent design. It really works. I loved watching someone come more alive, more vibrant, more in contact with their deeper self, more awakened to possibilities beyond what they knew. I still love this today!

Polarity is not about fixing anything, and this gave me the freedom to learn and explore. I didn't need to be right. If something wasn't resonating while I was working with someone, I could try something else. I stayed open and curious, paying attention to whether the life force was increasing in potency or decreasing. Those were my measures. I had an innate ability to sense energy. The skill most likely came from the ways I survived my trauma. I believe our ways of surviving can transform into great skills. I was relieved to play in learning. Societal programming puts so much pressure on us to get it right. We tend to lose playfulness, curiosity, and innocence in learning. When I began teaching, I wanted to ensure those qualities were at the heart of my practice.

At the end of the day, through my training, I acquired skills of stillness, receptivity, deep listening, discovery, and curiosity. These are valuable tools that have sustained me on my life journey of growing, healing, and being restored. They are the foundational skills I harvested through my beginning years of studying Polarity, worthy practices for ways of being and action. They are the bedrock of my life, my teaching, and my own evolution.

You too can cultivate your access to your own vital force with these skills. You will be restored in vision, thought, and heart to the true nature of who you are.

CHAPTER 7

MY LEGACY JOURNEY

Now is the time. I am ready to be visible about the force that restored me from my trauma. I am whole and holy and want everyone to have the opportunity to be restored into their true vibrancy, purpose, and liberation.

Being witnessed by my family while being raped made visibility seem dangerous to me.

Therefore, I have kept the power that I know through Polarity Therapy quiet to the world.

Now I am ready to shout from the mountaintops what I know and have experienced so others too can access the deepest and truest self they have, their own soul.

———

In my professional life, I'm known for my company UnifyingSolutions. My business is based on executive coaching, team and organizational development for organizations, and cultural competency for organizational success. In addition, I am a Master Somatic Coach and have certifications in the Enneagram,

FEBI Leadership Assessment Test, and DecisionWise 360 Assessment. I've had the good fortune of contributing to the AIDS community through AIDS Healing Weekends, as well as to sexual and domestic violence organizations and a leadership training program in a male prison for five years. I've designed public courses in women's leadership (Women Generating: Collective Power for Positive Change) and developed, with Dr. Sierra Austin-King and James A. White, Community Safe Conversations about Race. I'm grateful for the impact I've had on individuals, teams, organizations, and communities.

You might be thinking: What about Polarity? For decades, Polarity was a sidebar for me. Few in my professional networks knew about my work with Polarity. Plus, I didn't see a way to build a lucrative business with it. Still, I never stopped practicing Polarity. The thought nagged at me: I needed to find a way to continue the thread of Polarity Therapy in my life for myself and for people that were interested in learning about it. After all, Polarity was in my life to stay. It was and is the foundation of a path I have dedicated my life to.

Though I stopped my formal study of Polarity Therapy when I was twenty-four, I continued studying on my own, reading Dr. Stone's books and seeking to know the material inside of me. I wanted to take time to digest and integrate my learning. I *needed* time to deepen my understanding before I began teaching.

When I taught, I did not want my course to be a purely intellectual exercise. In other words, I didn't want to overwhelm students with static information. Nothing could be further from how I'd experienced Polarity. Instead, I wanted to teach a course rich with embodiment, one that also incorporated intellectual knowledge.

At twenty-eight, I offered my first Polarity Therapy Training. I knew I wanted to ensure that the most essential aspect of Polarity was present: We have a wireless design of an energy system operating in our body. This design gives our life a purpose beyond the material world of successes and failures. It gives us a pathway to know our deepest self, our soul consciousness, within.

From the start, my pedagogy was theme-focused. While Dr. Stone espoused many hands-on treatments in his books, I was not interested in training practitioners in Polarity Therapy. Instead, I wanted to support human beings who were hungry to find healing and grounded hope for themselves by learning about what was deep inside of them.

Over the next two decades, I taught many students in numerous modalities and formats. My own experience in Polarity classrooms informed my teaching style. I'd share a key truth of Polarity, invite everyone to sit with it, and see if we could find our own way of knowing. Then we'd do a hands-on treatment or discuss how to support our mind creating grooves that represent the truth about life. I included embodied practices, too, drawing from my work with choreographer and dancer Anna Halprin. I found ways to support people working with their resistance so that resistance became generative instead of immobilizing.

One such practice was creating a shape in the body that mimicked the resistance a person felt within themselves. There's a story, a narrative, a belief associated with that resistance, with that shape. My shape was collapsed, turned in on itself. It represented the self-hatred I'd felt for so long, the wanting to die. In class, I'd ask people to draw their shape, write the narrative on paper, and then become the shape. By fully investing in the shape, the posture that had been held was now met with acknowledgment. The shape would soften, unfurl, and transform into an emerging, life-giving shape. Afterward, I'd ask participants to write and draw the new emerging presence as well as the new narrative.

The class was always surprised by this exercise. Usually we fight against our resistance. We push it away, get angry at it, or hate it. Blending with it is a way to honor the intelligence of the resistance. Then beauty emerges like a sprouting seed. Having a new way of being can become one's North Star, rather than the limited thoughts associated with the wound. Rather than self-hatred being my North Star, my North Star became an affirmation: "I am a radiant soul, part of the source of life for all of creation." Repeating that made me inherently worthy. I did not have to earn my worth.

As I taught, I grew ever more creative. I evolved. Teaching allowed me to recognize more depth in myself as well as how I could support people in their own evolution and growth. Still, I never lost sight of a consistent truth: What would remain the same is that the source of life is inside of us. Our soul is a drop of the eternal ocean of love. In this life, we get the opportunity to learn about the wireless system of energy that is operating on our behalf. We get to decide if we want to become stewards of our own gift of life.

When I turned fifty, I decided to stop teaching Polarity. During that break, I studied Embodied Leadership at Strozzi Institute in Petaluma. That period of time afforded me the opportunity to grow personally and professionally. As I explored a new era of my life, I remembered those early days of attuning to nature while studying Polarity in Northern California. This reawakened my understanding that life is in everyone and everything.

Perhaps I wouldn't have returned to teaching if it weren't for my dear friend and teaching assistant, Anne Santilli. Anne insisted. I'd formed a racially diverse teaching team for a public course that I'd designed, Women Generating, and I wanted those instructors to build their capacity to stay present and hold space for their classes. Holding space requires deep, grounded presence and staying present over a long period of time. Anne, who knew about the role Polarity played in my life, said the only way they were going to increase their skill level would be if I taught.

And so I created a new curriculum. Here you have it. I began again.

https://unifyingsolutions.com/book

PART II

YOU:
YOUR
INHERENT
WIRELESS
DESIGN

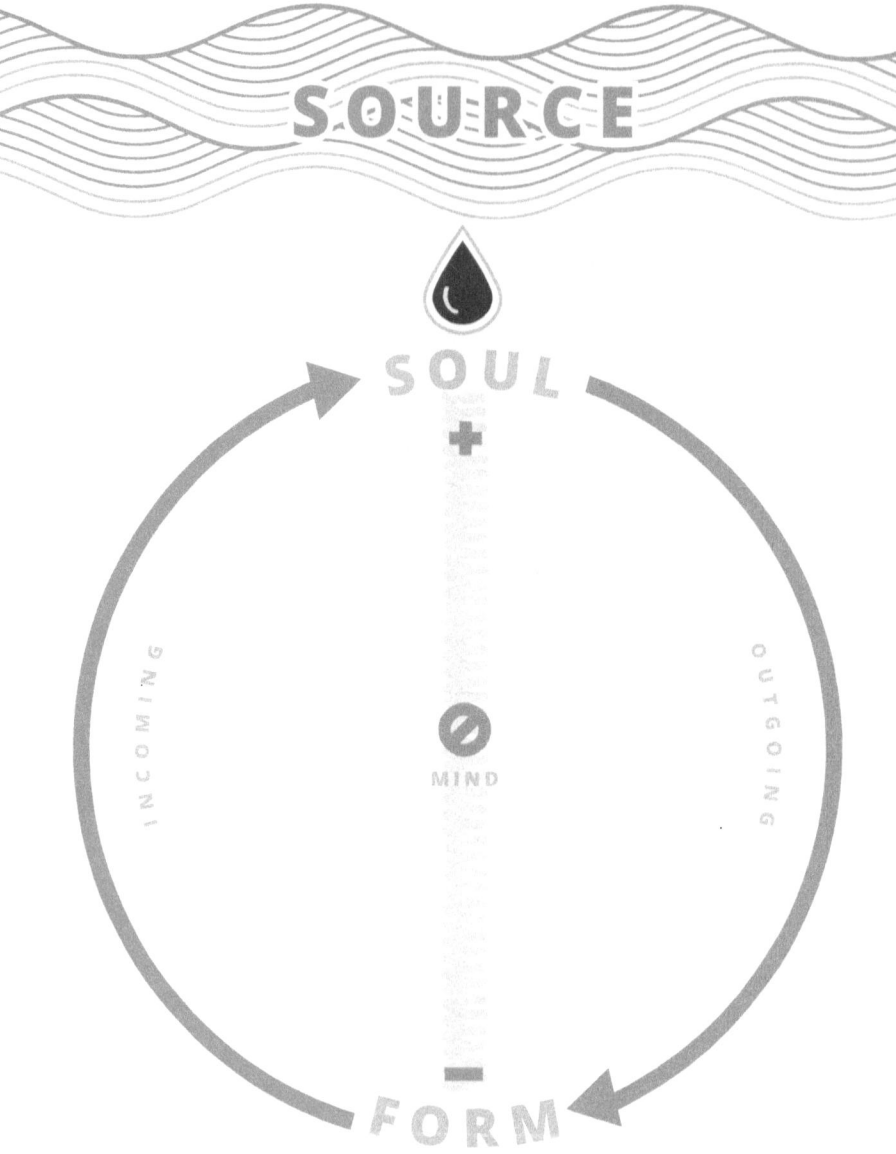

SOUL CONSCIOUSNESS OPERATING THROUGH FORM TO REMEMBER ITSELF.

https://unifyingsolutions.com/book/

SOURCE

SOUL

+

INCOMING

MIND

OUTGOING

FORM

SOUL CONSCIOUSNESS OPERATING THROUGH FORM TO REMEMBER ITSELF.

CHAPTER 8

YOUR INHERENT WIRELESS DESIGN

WHY DID NO ONE TELL ME THIS BEFORE?

There is a treasure hidden inside you, invisible to your eyes. This treasure may be unknown to you now, yet it is knowable within. What compels you to seek this treasure is the sense that there is something missing from your life, no matter your worldly successes and enjoyments.

Your treasure holds the keys to deeper vibrancy, purpose, liberation, resources, rest, connected relationships, and inherent value.

Your soul is your vital life force, and it is pulsing inside of you every moment. Your soul is waiting for your discovery.

You have everything you need inside of you to go on your treasure hunt within.

1. Longing: You ache to remember and return to your eternal essence.
2. Power to still your mind: You have the capacity to still your mind (not easy, but possible).

3. Discernment: You have the power of discernment, which provides you with internal guidance.

4. Agency: You have the agency to make life-giving choices.

—

The wireless energy system inside of you is your ideal template to serve you. It's also your ideal template to true you. By "true you," I mean what aligns with your deepest self. This system, and this template, are always available to you. Once you learn about the design, you have the opportunity to use it as a North Star, a guiding roadmap.

This vital life energy is a gift from the source of life for all of creation. We are not the initiators of our life energy. If we were, we could keep generating our life forever. We would never experience death. Death is promised to us after our first breath.

We are utterly dependent on the source of life for our very existence.

Dr. Stone says on page 35 in *Book 1,* "Creation would not survive, were it not constantly sustained by the outgoing breath of the ONE ETERNAL SOURCE of Energy, the Creator of all, in every realm of being."

We tend to think our treasures exist in the material world. Everything we acquire in the material world is temporary. This is hard to come to terms with. Our beloved relationships, pets, cars, homes, clothes, shoes—none of it comes with us when we die.

Within such a paradigm, seeking fulfillment from the material world makes no sense. The material world is fed by the same source as our very own life. Why not go directly to the source within us?

While we need to interact with the outside world to sustain the body through warmth, air, water, and food, what truly fulfills us is right inside of us.

You may not believe you have this inside of you. My history of trauma certainly prevented me from believing I had this capacity. You, too, might be living with doubts, a limited sense of self, and a fear that all this is possible for everyone but you. That is not true.

Your soul is pulsing inside of you at the center of your being at every moment.

BATTERY

The wireless design operates like a battery, a triune function of a positive and negative pole with a neutral gradient.

A battery has a sending positive pole that is received by a negative pole. The negative pole returns the energy to the positive pole with the same intensity of current, circuitry, and flow. Energy is movement between opposing poles with a neutral gradient.

The triune function of two poles with a neutral gradient operates in micro and macro levels of energy flow everywhere in this world of duality. Every cell in your body, the atoms of your cells, every aspect of life operates with this triune function. What this means is that energy is moving between poles in all of creation. Whether in the cells of your body or the cosmos, all of creation gets animated through energy.

YOUR IDEAL PATTERN—WIRELESS OPERATING DESIGN

The soul, a drop of the eternal ocean of love, is your positive pole. Your soul is your North Star, your guiding force. The positive pole, your soul, sends energy toward the negative pole, your body. With no interference, the sending current is immediately attracted back to itself. Thus, the soul will send a current through the form of the body to reunite with the positive pole, itself. This is magnetism.

Polarity Therapy is soul consciousness operating through form to remember itself. You are designed to know the truth of who you are as a radiant soul. The wireless system is simple, purposeful, and direct.

You are designed to have an inner birth of remembering your true self, your true nature, and your true value.

THE POSITIVE POLE

The soul only knows to send. The beloved only knows to love, impartially. The soul sends without bias, without judgment, without an agenda. The soul does not discriminate. Without interference, the return is also direct. The direct return is how we realize our birthright of knowing our own soul consciously.

THE NEGATIVE POLE

The negative pole of your body is meant to support your physiology, your chemistry, your structure. The body is inanimate without the vital energy of your soul. The vital soul current is independent of the body.

THE NEUTRAL GRADIENT

When the mind is neutral, there are no disturbing, disruptive thoughts. The mind is observing, witnessing, impartial, calm, curious, and open. It is a vessel for the soul to pass through.

The soul is meant to govern the mind and flow through the body. The negative pole, form, is not meant to become a place of fixation for either your identity or your fulfillment.

True fulfillment is found within.

The world of form is illusory by nature: It is constant moving energy, transitory, and ever changing. What animates form is eternal and unchanging. The only true satisfaction you will ever find is inside of you—your vibrant soul.

At some time in your life, you have had a moment of awe, an experience where time stands still. It might be witnessing a beautiful sunset, the sound of the ocean, the stillness in a forest, or a touching encounter. Everything stops for a moment. The mind is quiet. A deep, abiding aliveness emanates from within. There is no thought. Stillness and vibrancy. It's not only possible, but your birthright, to know this as your truth and power at all times. Imagine your life with greater access to this state of being more often. What more would be possible for you?

SUSTENANCE

The purpose of a battery is to conduct energy flow. In order to do so, it needs to be able to hold a charge—or, as with rechargeable batteries, to be recharged.

Human beings are constantly connected to an energy supply, a primal source of energy that provides life for all of creation. As long as your soul current is operating through your body, you are alive. When it withdraws from the body, we call this death, dust returning to dust. Genesis 3:19 says, "Dust you are and to dust you will return." Death makes this apparent. A few months ago, I witnessed this. I was with my goddaughter. Her father had recently passed away. As we sat together, she reflected, "We are truly just energy."

While we are alive, we have the opportunity to know this. We, too, are just energy. Energy lives through our body and our personality. In knowing this energy, we know ourselves. We do not take our personality with us when we die. Our soul leaves our body. Why not invest in your soul bank account?

As a drop of the source of life for all of creation, your soul contains the wisdom, brilliance, and knowledge of the source. Source intelligence runs through your body, keeping you alive.

REDEFINING HEALTH: A NEUTRAL MIND

We usually refer to our body as a measure of health. In this wireless energy system, we shift the definition of health to the vitality of your soul being free to run throughout your system. An uninterrupted flow.

With greater free flow, deep resource, rest, and equanimity will be available for whatever circumstances you face in the material world of form. There is a well of radiant resource to offer to what is happening at the surface in life. Without this anchor, you get tossed around in the tumultuous tides of life experiences; often, you are left drained.

Health is when we are in harmony with our life stream, the currency of our soul.

Health is when the mind is neutral.

Health is aligning the body, mind, and soul with the stream of life given by the Giver of Life.

Physical injuries have given me occasion to put this to the test. Recently, I fell while hiking the Appalachian Trail. I needed foot surgery, and two very large screws were awkwardly placed. They stayed there for months; then they had to be removed. During the procedures and during the healing, I felt grueling pain. It took a while to figure out how to manage the discomfort. The one thing I knew to do was to go deep inside myself, find the pulsing of my soul, and rest there. Then what was happening with my body seemed more distant, and I experienced peace inside of me. The "deeper than that" provided a resource for me in a very challenging experience.

INSPIRATION AND GUIDANCE IN REDEFINING HEALTH

When your mind is neutral, you are receptive to inspiration and wisdom from your soul consciousness. You receive guidance from the all-knowing, all-loving, unbiased consciousness of your vital soul.

A battery has a liquid medium for the current to run through. The liquid medium in our body is the cerebral spinal fluid.

The conduction of the energy of your soul emanates like the waves of oceanic tides through your cerebral spinal fluid. Your soul pulses inside you at the center of your being. As you read or listen to this book, your soul is pulsing. At each moment, you have the opportunity to turn your attention inward toward this radiant vibrancy. Your true nutrition is found here. Resting into your vitality is found here. Your only sustaining sense of wholeness and holiness is found here.

Through inner attentiveness and focus, it is possible to have access to your soul's vitality whenever you choose to.

Here is a recording for you to use at any time to practice being bathed by your own radiant life energy. The more you practice, the more you anchor yourself in the power that lives inside of you.

https://unifyingsolutions.com/book

HOW MY MOTHER FOUND HER INNER PEACE AT THE END OF HER LIFE

My mother believed that life was only physical, that nothing existed besides the here and now. She did not believe in God, nor did she believe in an afterlife. Her motto was: "What you see is what there is." It wasn't until she approached the last year of her life that she began to question her philosophy.

She'd been a highly successful doctor and had helped many people. She was one of a handful of women and the only Jewish woman in her medical school program. She was a pioneer and loved life; she loved the arts, travel, reading, people, history, clothes, causes, and more. For a long time, it was enough for her and sustained her. The world was her playground. She immersed herself in other cultures, drank in their art and history, and made best friends everywhere she went. Often, I was her companion on those adventures.

When she was eighty-eight, we went to Africa with a group of women to celebrate our friend's sixtieth birthday. My mother contracted walking pneumonia and stayed in a local village to recover. From the nurses attending to her, she learned that the young village women were unaware of condoms, and there was an upsurge in AIDS. She took it upon herself to ensure that these women had the means and skills to protect themselves. She asked for a banana and a condom and taught the village women how to put it on. They were so inspired that they asked if she would speak about AIDS to a seventh-grade rural classroom. While I was on a safari, she was having her own adventure.

As her activities became limited and the world slipped out of her grasp, she began to question what life was for. She longed to know something about her internal landscape and her inner world, which had gone unexplored.

On our adventures, my mother often commented on the calm I seemed to emanate. "There's something different about you," she might say, whether we were viewing elephants in the wild or comparing Uggs at Nordstrom. When she was around me, she seemed to slow down, to get still. She'd call me a lot when she was in a reactive state, trusting that I'd meet her with neutrality and honesty. She trusted the stillness that I cultivated in myself through Polarity.

I attribute my equanimity to my meditation practice. I'm as neurotic as anyone else, but I've chosen to dedicate my life to assisting my mind to become still so my trauma does not rule me.

As death approached, my mother was eager to know more about the atmosphere she sensed in me. She wanted to know about the emanating calm. One day she declared she wanted to learn to meditate. She did not have a lot of time to learn about peace, and she wanted to die peacefully.

She decided she wanted to become a Buddhist, and she wanted a teacher—NOW! My task was to find her a teacher with her requirements. Somehow, I found the perfect Buddhist teacher for my mom. God was not mentioned. The teacher spoke to my mom about death being just like any other transition; she shared a story about her college roommate who wanted to change schools. That roommate went to a new city and new college and had to adjust. This, the teacher shared, was what death was like. A change of location, a new place to grow accustomed to. My mom's fear of dying began to ease.

The teacher offered meditation practices that supported the transitory nature of death. Soon, my mother's meditation practice became the top priority in her life. With dedication, intensity of purpose, deep longing, and devoted application, she meditated to find the equanimity within. She had the most peaceful death I've ever witnessed, surrounded by all of her loved ones. I believe she was able to make that transition because she did her inner seeking and became healthy while dying.

My mom is the perfect example of following her longing to find peace within. You have the opportunity to do it now—why wait?

NEW PARADIGM FOR HEALTH

It is a wireless design that makes you human and gives you purpose. You did not create it. It is a gift given to you through your birth. Your heart does not beat without this current.

Everyone deserves to know what is operating inside of them. When introducing this design in the first Polarity class, I often hear people ask, "Why did no one tell me this before?"

This wireless system provides a pathway for you to come home to your deepest self. Your purpose for being alive moves from day-to-day reality (successes and failures, pain and pleasure) to an awakening to the radiance of your life current within, an inner birth acquainting you with your soul.

To begin to choose your soul consciousness requires an inner attentiveness and an inner seeking. The world of material form begins to no longer hold the same fascination as before. You will start to understand that what you are seeking is not sustainable in the outside world.

Most of us have had a nagging feeling that there is something missing. Perhaps you have felt an aching for deeper meaning or a yearning to access yourself in a different way. No matter how many successes you've had, no matter how many experiences you've had, no matter how many relationships you've had, no matter how many great meals you've had, there is an ache, an itch for something more. We name that longing.

Longing is within you. It's a hunger to awaken to your own soul vitality. You're being called home, to return and remember your inherent wholeness, your holiness.

Understanding this design demystifies what seems intangible. It makes the infinite practical.

To watch a teaching video of
Your Ideal Pattern Wireless Energy System,
go to https://youtu.be/Kqhi2xClbcE.

WHEN THE MIND BECOMES THE POSITIVE POLE.

CHAPTER 9

THE MIND BECOMES THE POSITIVE POLE

FROM FRIEND TO FOE

The mind has a role to play in our human experience. The purpose is to support our soul living in our physical body. An often-quoted statement from the Jesuit priest Pierre Teilhard de Chardin signifies this role: "We are not human beings having a spiritual experience. We are spiritual beings having a human experience."

Our neutral mind is our best friend. It's receptive to the guiding force of our higher mind, our soul consciousness. Our neutral mind is curious, observing, non-reactive, unbiased, quiet, still, and open. In *Book 3*, Volume 1, Stone writes of the healthy mind being the "neutral agent of the very Essence of matter in motion."

However, often, neutrality is not the first attribute that we assign to our mind. More likely, we think of our mind as being reactive, judging, intolerant, biased, right (which makes the other people or ideas wrong), defensive, or ego-centered.

The mind loses neutrality when it starts to take over as the positive pole, replacing the natural position of the soul. Different spiritual teachers have stated "the mind itself assumed the role of the Creator and Sustainer, and it is the mind which prompts one to go astray." And this is true. When the mind loses the guidance, wisdom, and knowledge from our higher self, we end up confused, frustrated, and suffering.

We spend most of our life completely unaware and unconscious of our mind becoming the dictator driving our own misery. Some of the ways our mind leads us astray are:

- Seduction by the senses
- Designing agendas (without the influence of the higher self)
- Leading with bias
- Outward seeking for fulfillment
- Building identity by virtues of righteousness, attachment, and pride
- Seeking safety, belonging, dignity, value, and connection from the world

WHAT HAPPENS TO OUR ATTENTION WITH THE MIND?

Attention is a soul quality. Our mind directs our attention. The first time I read in Dr. Stone's writing that attention is a soul quality, I paused. Previously, I assumed the mind generated our attention, but while researching attention, I found that it's described as focus; neuroscientists do not designate one specific site in the brain that controls attention. However, the brain has centers for focusing attention. Therefore, our mind dictates how we focus our attention. The dynamic movement of energy from pole to pole (positive and negative) is the strongest current in our body. Tuning into the power generated by the current gives us our sense of well-being and vibrancy. The mind determines the generating power between the poles. The more neutral the mind is, the more life-giving the energy is. When the mind is less neutral, the energy lessens and becomes dull.

Imagine a garden hose hooked up to an outdoor faucet, prepared to water your garden. When you turn on the hose, water comes out the other end with the pressure generated from the faucet. If you poke holes in the garden hose, water will leak out, and the water coming out the end will trickle instead of pour. That is exactly what happens to us when we "leak" our energy due to our mind. The mind diverts attention due to our senses, our attachments, our agendas, our outward seeking. With the leakage, we experience less vibrancy, less well-being, less free flow.

When I was in my mid-thirties, I facilitated healing weekends quarterly for the HIV/AIDS community with the Ohio Aids Coalition. I was living in Columbus, Ohio, at the time, and I was invited to facilitate workshops about Polarity Therapy, Healing the Child Within, and Mindfulness. Every Saturday night, we'd have an entertainment event. One weekend, we had a dance. I love to dance. One of the participants was a ballroom dance teacher, and eventually we found one another on the dance floor. Having been in the dance department at The Ohio State University, I had natural rhythm and grace in my movements. He asked me if I knew ballroom dancing, which I didn't, but he invited me to dance anyway. He promised to lead me, asking me to just let go. He was such an expert guide, and I gave myself over to him. Before I knew it, I was being twirled, dipped, and swept across the dance floor. It was thrilling! We were both high on endorphins afterwards.

I didn't see my dance partner again until the next healing weekend three months later. I was standing in the lobby of the retreat center when he entered. I was transfixed by him. There was so much light coming out of his eyes, so much radiance. We embraced. I told him how wonderful he looked. He was surprised, as he shared with me that he was dying. He told me he had been meditating, eating well, and sharing love with his partner, yet nothing would stop the progression of his disease. I asked him how he was with all of it, and he was sad and accepting. It is possible to be both. I asked him if I could comment on his radiance. He consented. I shared that I could witness the results of his efforts meditating, loving, and being loved. I told him how I was galvanized by the radiance exuding from him. I shared what I knew about health from Polarity. Health is being in tune with the energy current of our soul, not what is happening in our body. I saw the light of his soul through his eyes and was so moved. To me, he signified true health. We wept. I asked him what he thought happened at death. He spoke about his soul leaving his body. I stated that he was finding the treasure within now and that would go with him at the time of death. We hugged again.

Here was an important reminder for me about the truth of health in the energy system of Polarity. To me, he was fully alive. There are so many people walking around with healthy physical bodies in the world that are dull, lacking radiance, and not emanating a current of love. He taught me so much in that moment. I share this story in every Polarity class I teach.

In the following overview, I'll explore some of the ways the mind leads us astray. I include resources and neuroscience-based research for greater depth and understanding. The goal is to help you reflect on how these forces operate and to give you pause as you consider the power they hold.

THE SENSES

It's easy to see how the mind changes polarity when governed by the senses of taste, touch, smell, sight, and hearing. Our senses are the first engagement we have with the physical world. As our senses get more and more engaged with the material world, we become less and less aware of the energy within. Our attention becomes outwardly directed, and we lose soul inspiration.

Yet physical matter, while seemingly solid, is actually slowed down energy in motion. All material substance is energy moving between poles, just at different vibrations. Because we're unable to detect the dynamic movement of energy in matter, we assume physical matter is real. We lose awareness of the energy that animates matter.

Here's the conundrum:

I touch my arm; it feels solid. I sit in a chair; it feels solid. I smell chocolate chip cookies baking; the smell is delightful and enticing. I see a magnificent sunset; I am enthralled. I hear Nina Simone sing; I am touched. I eat that chocolate chip cookie; I am happy. Someone shares a tender story with me; I am internally moved. Lovely. Yet all these experiences are temporary and fleeting. My arm or the chair, while both feel solid, are atoms in motion. I don't detect that motion, that moving energy. I take it as it appears to me. Soon, I begin searching for ways to replicate the feelings evoked through my senses. While pleasurable, these feelings are temporary. My valiant efforts result in more and more seeking. Seeking becomes endless.

For a long while, dear friends of mine waxed poetic about the Banoffee Pie they'd eaten in England and Wales. Ten years later, I met up with them in London for a meditation retreat. We decided it was time for me to try Banoffee Pie. Off we went on a rainy, cold day in search of the elusive pie. We did research, followed leads, only to end up pie-less after a six-hour pursuit. Finally, we caught word of a vegan restaurant that had the pie. We called and ended up there for dinner. Their rendition of Banoffee Pie was raw, all dates and nuts, certainly not the butter-laden creation we'd hoped to devour. Looking back, I can't believe we spent a day in a city I love for its history, art, and theater chasing Banoffee Pie. How easy it is to get caught up in pursuit of a fanciful whim and wind up utterly distracted and consumed.

(I eventually did try a proper slice in the English countryside while at an obscure Chinese restaurant. Often things come to us when we are not frantically searching for them. The pie was good, but by that time, the hype overrode the glory.)

AGENDAS

We need agendas; we need outlines; we need steps. I have made so many agendas for facilitating trainings and relied on them.

The agendas I'm talking about are the agendas your mind makes that drive limiting choices. Limiting choices are those that might diminish you, devalue you, or work against you.

Creating attachments to outcomes limits your growth and possibilities. When you want something so badly that you place your value on it, you wind up disappointed when that want isn't achieved or obtained. The mind starts dictating what it thinks you need while also driving you to find your value in the external world. Neither work on your behalf.

Being filled with self-hatred from my trauma, I believed I was unlovable. In order to seem lovable, I began seeing the needs in other people and serving those needs, all the while ignoring my own. My mind created the agenda of sacrificing myself for others to get stroked with positivity. Here was proof that I was lovable from the outside. Only, this agenda failed me. Often, I'd end up not only exhausted but completely depleted. My lovability wasn't anchored inside of me. The more I treasured my life, the more I considered my needs. The more I experienced the pulsing, radiant energy inside of me, the more I understood that my worthiness resided inside of me. Self-sacrifice no longer became the positive pole of my mind. My worth became my positive pole.

BIAS

Bias is a part of our human experience. *Collins Dictionary* defines it as "a tendency to prefer one person or thing to another, and to favor that person or thing."

Our preferences are subjective and personal. We often unthinkingly identify with our biases. Consider people who prefer Coke over Pepsi, or the other way around. My husband is committed to Diet Coke as his preference. (Yes, everyone who knows him or knows his preference has sent him research and data about Diet Coke. He has the information and just loves his Diet Coke.) If he discovers that an establishment does not carry Coke products, he's less likely to return. His bias determines where he invests his dollars.

Psychology Today defines bias as "a tendency, inclination, or prejudice toward or against something or someone," a "cognitive shortcut." We all have these inclinations and take these cognitive shortcuts. After all, bias developed throughout our evolution as a way to protect us as we navigate our world.

Psychology Today goes on to write of biases:

Some biases are positive and helpful—like choosing to only eat foods that are considered healthy or staying away from someone who has knowingly caused harm. But biases are often based on stereotypes, rather than actual knowledge of an individual or circumstance. Whether positive or negative, such cognitive shortcuts can result in prejudgments that lead to rash decisions or discriminatory practices.

We are a conglomeration of biases, both useful and unuseful. Sometimes they even contradict one another. For example, an alcoholic might simultaneously have a preference to get sober and the uncontrollable urge to reach for another drink.

Biases become a concern when we don't see the way our stereotypes impact us. Social systems of dominance and oppression influence—even infiltrate—our minds and prejudice us toward stereotypical preferences. These social systems create hierarchical values for different groups of people; those values advance certain groups and disadvantage others. It's important to remember that these value structures are not based on the reality that life is in everyone and everything. The source of life sends unbiased energy to everyone and all forms of life in creation; it's the vital energy that unites rather than divides us. And yet, throughout history, groups of people have dehumanized other groups of people to have an advantage.

Biases of dehumanization prohibit all human beings from accessing resources and opportunities, thus inhibiting the collective community's ability to become a vibrant world. When the mind is the positive pole, operating with these biases can lead to external and internal harm. In the United States, gender, class, race, and religion are major factors in determining who has access to power and opportunity. Consider an issue such as wage disparity, whether by gender or race. According to Statista, there is no U.S. state where women out-earn men. Statista also finds the Black population has the lowest median household income. This research shows the power of bias when the mind is operating as the positive pole. The gender and race-gap research are evidence of social systems developing practices out of bias.

This can also happen at an individual level. Through class, race, age, weight, ability, religion or any other ism, a person might be overlooked for a position of advancement due to stereotypes. To overcome bias requires an interest in examining where it comes from. One book that has been critical in helping me understand bias is *Biased, Uncovering the Hidden Prejudices That Shape What We See, Think, and Do* by Jennifer Eberhardt, a social psychologist who is currently a psychology professor at Stanford University. Through education and intentionality, we can create a more equitable world where every life matters.

OUTER SEEKING VS. INNER SEEKING

Back to the battery, the ideal wireless system. The positive pole sends an outgoing current that becomes the incoming current at the negative pole. Sending and returning. Energy in motion between two poles. This operating system is designed to support you connecting with your own soul within. Longing is the inherent attribute of the incoming current, creating an inner attentiveness.

We yearn to seek inside because we sense there is something other than what the material world offers. Our sustainable fulfillment lies inside of us with the light of the soul. Our longing creates a hunger to seek within where our fulfillment, nourishment, and resource resides. Our longing is our ache of homesickness that arises when we're not at one with our soul consciousness.

However, the minute we take our first breath, we begin moving our attention away from pure consciousness and attending to the material. Over time, we try to find fulfillment outside of ourselves.

We look outward to validate, to prove our value, worth, purpose, and happiness. Trying to define ourselves from external feedback—whether it be work, relationships, or society—leaves us at the mercy of these forces. Everything outside of us is subjective and changeable. We are in danger when we put ourselves at the whims of other people and social constructs. These are all limited perspectives from individual minds and collective thought based on biases. No one has the right to tell you your value. No society, no person, no job, no anything has that right. The truth is you *already* are worthy and valuable. You are alive, here, because you have been given the gift of life from the source of life. The power of radiant life is inside of you. You don't have to do anything to earn it or deserve it. It's already given to you. You're inherently whole and holy. Originating from this reality, you get to determine who you are from the inside of you. It is wonderful to have supportive people around you committed to what is inside of you.

Desire is a different beast than longing. Desire is driven by the mind, and it craves solutions in the material world. When the mind is directed by these desires, outward seeking goes on auto-pilot. The attention gets stuck seeking in the material world and begins to thwart the impulse of inner seeking. The lack of deeper contact with the vibrancy of the current of life takes away our sense of well-being.

The desires I'm talking about are differentiated from our true heart desires, those desires inspired by our inner knowing. Becoming willful with craving for things, people, outcomes, and other desires driven through egoic interests of greed, attachment, and pride misguide us. Ultimately, their pursuit leads us to frustration and suffering. As an Executive Coach, I've seen people strive for a position to prove their value. If something interrupts that positionality, whether not being offered a position or losing a position, their sense of value is greatly impacted. The ego takes a hit. If your value is based solely on external circumstances, you've lost your sense of self within. It's wise to make your best effort and leave the results to the forces at hand without your value being dependent on those forces.

The mind is limited compared to soul consciousness. When given free rein to dictate the course of our life, to determine our value, it does so from a limited and misguided perspective. In trying to find fulfillment and validation from an ever-changing material world, we will meet dead ends, frustration, and, ultimately, suffering. We spend most of our life completely unaware and unconscious of the distortion of our mind becoming the dictator driving our own misery.

Hunger is associated with both longing and desire. Longing is a hunger for reunion with our deepest self, whereas desire is the mind tricking us to try to fill that hunger in the material world. When we interrupt the autopilot compulsion of the mind misguiding us, we have the freedom to follow our own longing.

Desires and cravings may seem endless. Still, we can thwart them by asking ourselves some key questions:

- Is my happiness dependent on the outcome alone?

- Am I okay making my best effort not knowing or being able to control the outcome?
- Am I listening to my deepest self or what society thinks is right and good?
- Do I know my own internal value independent of the outcome?

This isn't to say that we don't experience disappointment when we don't get what we want. However, we want to be sure we have our inner resource to face disappointment and the willingness to move forward with whatever is next.

We want our desires to serve our inner truth. Our sense of self will always be limited through the lens of our mind. Yet hidden in matter is ultrasonic energy that pervades all of life. Invisible and mysterious, it is the sustainer of all living form. Our inner seeking rewards us with the greatest riches; our outer seeking ultimately leaves us bankrupt.

SAFETY

Another way the mind leads us astray is by seeking our safety and belonging solely through an outer lens.

There's never a guarantee of safety in the world. Never. "Safety" is the condition of being free from risk or harm. Now pause: Have you ever lived free from harm or risk? I certainly haven't. To hope for safety at all times is unrealistic. Within marginalized communities that are already at risk, safety is not even remotely possible. When I teach, I tell the class that we ought to all lie down right now and give up if we think we're going to find safety in the world.

I believe safety can only truly exist inside of ourselves, at the center of our being. Our living vital energy is safe, ever-giving, never putting us in harm's way or at risk. Our inner energy generates love, grace, and mercy. Learning to rest inside, being resourced by this radiant energy, is inner safety.

My dear friend, Polarity Teaching Assistant, and human extraordinaire, Sharonda Crome, has two African-American sons. She knows their risk walking out the door, with the world criminalizing Black men. According to the NAACP, one in three black men can expect to go to prison in their lifetime. Sharonda has taught her sons to know their safety and value within. She reminds them of their inherent dignity. She wants them walking out the door with that inner knowing when they are up against such a disturbing statistic.

BELONGING

Belonging is a basic human need. We all want to belong to someone, something, some group. In seeking belonging, we hope for feelings of familiarity, comfort, security, and affinity.

Searching for a sense of external belonging leaves us at the mercy of outside forces. In order to find a way to belong, people often adapt by conforming to a person, group, or community. They abandon their deepest self, all in the hope of finding an elusive sense of comfort and security. Who determines the values and rules that say any of us can belong? The rules can always change.

One place we see challenges with belonging is the workplace. Many work environments have not done due diligence to create cultures that support racial, ethnic, religious, gender identity, and/or class difference(s) so that everyone feels included, secure, and comfortable. People who don't identify with the dominant culture work hard to find ways to belong. Imagine having to spend your workday in a place where you are not fully valued. Imagine having your contributions minimized; imagine being required to prove yourself over and above the standards—and still it's never enough. The hope of comfort and security is elusive. Your basic need is not getting met. When I coach people facing these obstacles at work, they share their deep exhaustion.

Seeking belonging solely outside of yourself can be concerning, especially when the world is not designed to include you, let alone support your thriving. At best, the world provides an inconsistent sense of belonging. Often, looking for belonging in the world leads to disappointment and hurt. After all, our social systems of dominance and oppression are prevalent in every aspect of civic engagement, leaving many people empty. And while many feel a pressing need to find affinity outside of work, even those affiliations are subject to change and unpredictability.

Learning to rely on your life currency within gives you the anchor of inner belonging. This internal resource is unchanging. You deserve to experience comfort and security from within. The radiant current of your soul is unchanging. It never leaves you. There is nothing you have to prove or earn to belong to the life within. Eternal comfort resides within.

MIND RETURNING TO THE MIND

When the mind takes charge as the positive pole, it sends and returns to itself. The thoughts of our mind dominate, and without guidance from the higher self, are left to wreak havoc.

Think of the notion of behavioral confirmation. According to *Neurolaunch*, "At the heart of behavioral confirmation lies the concept of self-fulfilling prophecies. It's a bit like a social feedback loop: our expectations shape our behavior, which influences others' responses, which in turn reinforce our initial expectations. It's a cycle that can be hard to break, especially when we're not aware it's happening."

As a young person, my mind fixated on hating myself and being unlovable. My behavior was that of being overly generous in order to get feedback and proof that I was lovable. I put that responsibility on someone else when it wasn't their job. When anyone didn't give me the response I hoped for or was seeking, in a way only I knew would work, I got confirmation I was unlovable. That led me down the rabbit hole of shame and self-hatred.

The mind's perspective is limited. It mimics a computer's operating system, which functions how it's programmed to. We have no idea of the scope of programming that occurs in our minds. While computers are supposed to have users to work the programming, our mind is the user. The mind, on the other hand, guides on its own. It becomes the user and the programming.

THE BATTERY AND THE MIND

The positive pole is the superconscious mind, the higher self.

The position of neutrality is the conscious mind.

The negative pole is the unconscious mind.

If the neutral position of the mind is the conscious mind, then choices and decisions are able to be made consciously with the superconscious mind, and the higher self is the guide and influence.

The unconscious mind can be used for the sustenance of our body. For example, we don't think in order to digest our food. Our physiology is designed to support the functionality of our body without thought. We don't think to breathe. We might need to remind ourselves to take a deep breath if our breathing has become shallow due to a startle or a habitual response to trauma. When startled, our sympathetic nervous system kicks in by going into fight-or-flight mode. Many people never fully recover from the startle response and perpetually breathe shallowly. When we become aware that we want deeper, more productive breathing that reflects a parasympathetic state, we can consciously choose to do so. That's because the conscious mind has decided it wants more for ourselves than just surviving. We were breathing without thought, and we wanted more for ourselves. We must choose that.

Trauma is digestible. Traumatic experiences are not permanent. They happen. We react to them. We can learn about our reactions and eventually choose a different outcome. The experience is no longer happening in present time. We want to use our conscious mind to apply our internal, birthright wisdom to remember the truth of who we are underneath the traumatic experience. The heartbeat of our own soul always pulses within—it was pulsing before the trauma, during the trauma, and after the trauma.

However, our undigested trauma gets held in the unconscious mind. The unconscious mind gets weighted down, burdened, by the undigested material. It becomes hard for the unconscious parasympathetic processes to function as fully as possible to support our functionality. Thus, trauma has a physiological response within the body. When the mind gets bonded to the traumatic response and starts leading with that reaction, we are left adrift. The positive pole of the soul struggles to lead us to restoration.

It's crucial to understand the role of the mind in determining our access or lack of access to a vibrant, purposeful, and liberated life. Allowing the mind to become the dictator, creator, and sustainer doesn't serve us. Understanding the power of the mind gives us choice; we determine its role in our health, well-being, and equanimity.

To watch a teaching video of
When You Mind Becomes the Positive Pole,
go to https://youtu.be/twlYg9Vd7FM.

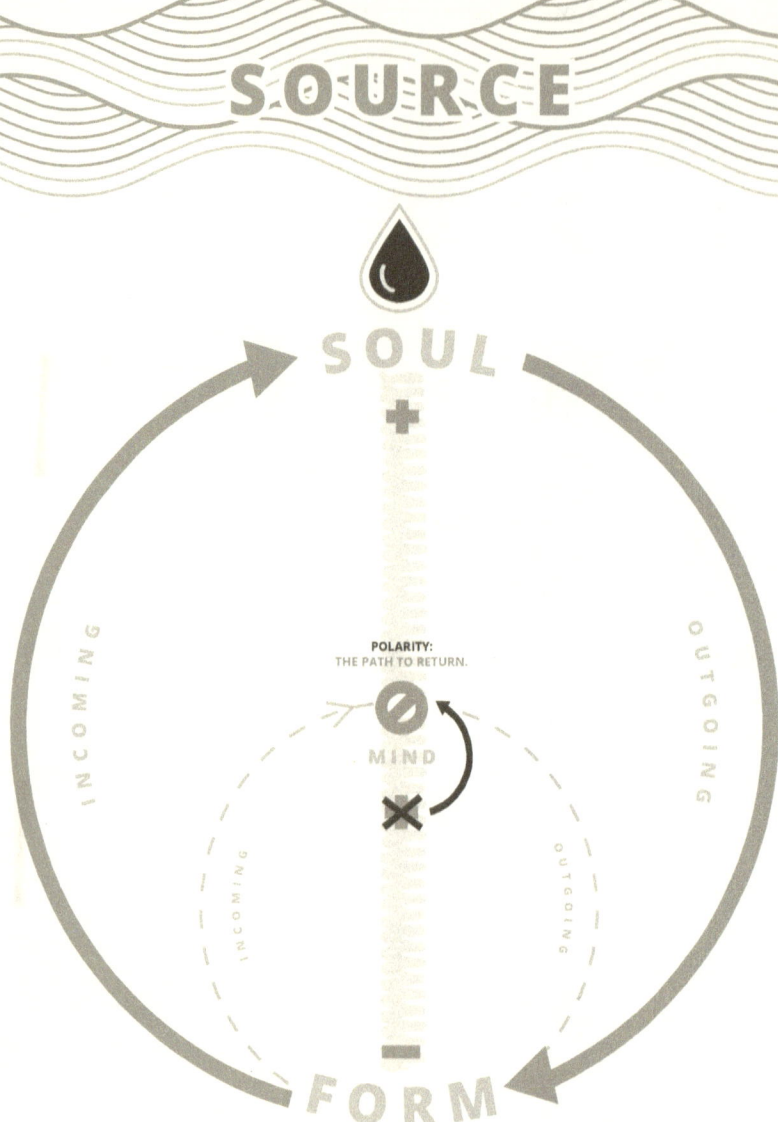

SOURCE

SOUL

+

POLARITY:
THE PATH TO RETURN.

MIND

INCOMING

OUTGOING

INCOMING

OUTGOING

—

FORM

THE PATH OF POLARITY IS THE MIND TURNING TO NEUTRALITY.

CHAPTER 10

THE PATH OF POLARITY

RETURNING THE MIND TO NEUTRAL

The path of Polarity is a lifelong journey of returning the mind toward neutrality, reversing it from being the positive pole to its original design. Doing so provides purpose and direction for the human experience. The reward of slowly stilling the mind brings you closer to becoming conscious of your inner radiance, your true self. This is consciousness operating through form to remember itself.

The journey becomes one of slowly turning the attention inward, withdrawing the attention away from the material world of form to the formless within. Knowing the animating energy inside you and all of creation becomes the focus of the search and the reward.

Along the dedicated path of Polarity, the mind becomes more impartial, unbiased, clear focused, accepting, and humble. The more attuned we are to the life energy within, the more we become aware that we're interrelated. We humanize across our differences and begin to see life in everyone and everything. By doing so, we reduce harm, instead generating positivity and possibility.

The body we occupy is temporary. The identity of our personality and ego are temporary. It's as if our soul went to a car lot and picked out a car with certain color schemes and amenities. The soul got into the car to go on a journey of knowing its own radiance. The soul had a clear destination. However, another driver, the mind, came along and hijacked the car, holding the soul hostage. The mind took the soul on a wild goose chase. The driver of the car has no clear direction of where to go or for what reason. It keeps driving, chasing experiences, always running out of gas. Eventually, the car will die. The hope is that, before death, the soul gets the opportunity to drive the car again, restoring the initial purpose of knowing itself.

The current of life energy flows inside at all times, from pole to pole. Pulsing, vibrating at the very center. Life is happening right inside, like a waterfall coursing through the center of your being. Life is happening. Your attention can be with the waterfall of vital energy or at the surface of ever changing experiences. (One potential title for this book was: Life's Happening, Where Are You?)

The more neutral the mind becomes, the more the soul begins to govern the mind again. Soul qualities of acceptance, grace, wisdom, patience, tolerance, and kindness become North Stars for the mind. Over time, the mind learns to become a humble servant to the soul. That's the ideal path to follow. The process of making the mind neutral is not easy, yet it's a worthy pursuit. Greater vibrancy, freedom, equanimity, resource, and harmony become available along the path of remembering and returning to the power of life within.

I see Polarity as a path. In the *Merriam-Webster Dictionary*, path is defined as "a way of life, conduct, or thought." Exactly! When you view Polarity as a path, it becomes a way of life, a way to conduct your behavior and actions in alignment with your deepest self. Soul qualities will govern your thoughts. Choice is now available. It's up to each one of us to either make life-giving choices or those that siphon energy from the wellspring of life. Achieving perfect neutrality at all times is rare. Saints achieve this state of consciousness. Yet it is possible to dedicate yourself to this path, making the truth of who you are within as your life purpose. As you travel this path, you will experience more and more moments of greater depth and stillness. There is an eternal wellspring inside to explore and know awaiting you.

The path is slow. You might follow it for a whole lifetime. This is a rare opportunity. We live in a world that seeks immediate feedback and results. The hunger for deeper meaning, deeper connection, and deeper taste of inner currency provides the fuel for a dedicated practice. This is not a journey of flashy, temporary results. This is a journey of sustainable, long-lasting rewards. Understanding how the operating wireless system works becomes a scientific design to guide you. The purpose of awakening to your radiance within calls you.

When I was studying Polarity, I needed to validate that the operating system was true inside of me. I wanted to know how I experienced a dynamic current running between two poles with a neutral gradient. As I previously shared, it was through lying on the earth, harmonizing with nature, that I could feel a pulsing inside of me. I was not creating it. It was already given to me for me to know. In that moment, I was able to pause, quiet my mind, and experience a potent vibrancy within. I felt safe, connected, belonging, held, and valued.

We need both a roadmap and experiences that compel us to practice and find the power of that current within. Without validating experiences, the wireless system is just a theoretical model.

I believe the soul guides us to inner experiences throughout our lives. As a child, I sought a way to find freedom in myself. I was looking for spaciousness, holiness. On this quest, the cupboard in my closet became a sanctuary. Just inside my closet, the cupboard had doors that opened from the middle. It was hidden by clothes that hung on two racks, one on top of the other. I had to move them aside to access the cupboard doors. This required that I exert force, opening those doors against the clothes. Inside the cupboard, I found refuge, hiding from danger and violence, not wanting to be noticed or found. When I was small, I could curl my body under a shelf, comforted and contained. As I got older, I had to remove the shelf so my growing body could fit. In the darkness, I found stillness. Tucked away in there, no one noticed I was missing. It was quiet. I could hear my breath and feel my heartbeat. Everything seemed to stop, and yet at the same time, everything came alive. While my body was curled in on itself, something inside me released and uncurled. I felt safe. I loved the feeling of being hidden. I reveled in the spaciousness within me. I felt alive and holy. I knew that when I exited, I'd be forced to become vigilant, small, full of self-hatred, and terrified.

I believe my heroines Grace, Love, and Mercy led me to that cupboard. Some impulse was working inside of me, for me. It called to me from the depths in my darkest hour. Below cognition, I responded to an impulse to seek something restorative. That's life at its greatest.

Turning one's attention inward is a valiant undertaking. Working to still the mind is a valiant undertaking. And yet it can be terrifying to admit that the material world is an illusion, that the ego serves as a defense for the belief that you're a separate individual. It can be daunting to surrender what you've thought to be true and turn inward. The word "*surrender*" may roll off the tongue, but putting it into action is terrifying for most of us. We need to proceed slowly so we can handle it and not freak out. If you place a silk cloth on a rose bush, you don't want to rip it off all at once. It will absolutely shred the piece of fabric. Removing it one thorn at a time keeps the cloth intact. Yes, there will be small holes and a few minor rips, but the silk will be in one piece. We, like the cloth, want to remain whole while we practice dying to the illusion of the material world while also releasing the false notion that we are separate. Dispelling illusion is hard.

If we are not truly separate, being united by the source as our supply, what does that say about our uniqueness? We have value in our unique and authentic expression. A seed has a potential expression, bursting forth from the vital energy within. Broccoli produces broccoli, squash produces squash, zinnia seeds produce zinnias. Each of us has a unique expression, a unique value, and a unique talent hidden in our seed of life.

Life unites; ego divides. In the divisiveness, comparison creates competition, hierarchy, defensiveness, righteousness, and estrangement from soul qualities. It's exhausting. So much energy is required to uphold the ego or seek fulfillment (and value and purpose) from the material world. At some point, if you are lucky, the fatigue informs you that these efforts are wasted pursuits. A void—emptiness—emerges. Who are you if your identity is no longer rooted in the outside world? Through stilling your mind, you discover your deepest self.

STILLING THE MIND

There is a great quote by Paracelsus, a sixteenth-century German-Swiss physician and alchemist who established the role of chemistry in medicine. He said, "Man is ill because he is never still." (This quote from the 1500s reflects the time. In class, I update it by saying, "Human beings are ill because they are never still.") Like Dr. Stone, Paracelsus defines illness as coming from disturbances of the mind. Yes, everything refers back to the mind.

As we define it in Polarity, health is achieved through disciplining the mind to become still. This lifelong practice requires dedication and perseverance. Deciding what you want for yourself by keeping the goal in mind makes it possible.

STEPS TO STILLING THE MIND

There is no way to still the mind without a sitting, or mindfulness, practice. Some sort of meditation is necessary. The mind needs a break from itself to gain some quiet. Moving meditation is useful. However, I find having to sit with myself and sit through discomfort to find stillness works the best for me. I figure I'm going to have to face myself when I die; I might as well do it now. I want all of me integrated into my wholeness. Sometimes that means facing something uncomfortable inside. Maybe I wasn't as kind as I could have been. Maybe I was in a shame spiral. If I sit long enough, these nagging thoughts dissipate, and I am left with resonance to what restores me. I am also guided to accountability for action if needed. The mind is not my truth. What is deep inside of me is true. I have to sit to have access to my treasure within. True, I have been sitting for many, many years. I will continue to sit. I find it a time for inner sanctuary and reprieve from the world.

What's tricky, though, is trying not to fight the mind for control. It will react like a rebellious teenager. It will spar. It's best to avoid getting in power struggles with your mind. Instead, give it something else to do that serves you.

I gained important insight on this matter from the Buddhist teacher who worked with my mother at the end of her life. If you recall, my mom wanted to find peace and equanimity before she died. She urged me to find her a teacher as soon as possible. My research brought me to an incredible woman, a Buddhist meditation teacher. The teacher explained to my mom that death was a transition like any transition in life and that she could rely on her past experiences with transitions as strength to face the upcoming transition. According to the teacher, the mind resembles an infinite train that never stops moving. She encouraged my mom to visualize sitting in her car at a railroad track where the arm is down, the lights are flashing, and the infinite train is going by. The teacher instructed her to witness the train going by. If she got fascinated with any of the cars of the train and found herself exiting the car to join the train, she told her to come back in the car and observe the train. She said she most likely would have to do it over and over again. My mom found a way to use part of her attention to imagine an action that would limit her engagement with the ongoing mind. The mind does what the mind does: ongoing thinking. This practice provided a pause, a choice, and something else to focus the mind on that gave her space and stillness. The teacher didn't recommend stopping the train. We can't stop the mind from thinking. What we can do is determine what we want our thoughts to be and interrupt the grooves in our mind that distract us from our wholeness and holiness.

In my own experience, I needed a different mental groove to save and restore me from the deluge of self-hatred. If I tried to tell my self-hatred to stop without another thought to guide me, it would just intensify. When I learned about the ideal wireless system, I repeated to myself on a daily basis that there is radiant energy inside of me, my soul, given to me as a gift from the source of life for all creation. The repetition created new grooves in my mind. These grooves needed as much repetition as my self-hatred grooves; eventually, they became my deeper grooves. Fifty-two years later, my mind constantly hums with those words reverberating inside of me. I hear them. They restore me; they guide me. They are there for me when I lose my way, when I get triggered. The recovery time from being lost or triggered has lessened, and the inner anchor of self-love is moored deep within me.

If you visit unifying solutions.com/book, you'll enter the book portal where you'll find a sitting practice based on life energy.

I do this every day, multiple times a day. I love it.

I start with honoring the life I've been given by the source of life. Pause. Drink that in. I remind myself that my soul is pulsing through my cerebral spinal fluid at the center of my being. Pause. Drink that in. I imagine a tree of choice, or some aspect of nature that I cherish, and place it against my spine. Then I sit down and place my back against the tree and rest. I ask for my soul to bathe me and restore me. I sit. My mind is busy. This many years later my mind still chatters. I just don't find it interesting. I'm much more interested in the power of my own soul bathing me. I feel humbled and grateful beyond words. I never tire of this, ever. To have access to this knowledge and experience touches me deeply. I get to spend some of my time here on earth knowing the glory of who and what I truly am. The strength of my practice allows me access to this depth inside of me while I am coaching, hiking, cooking, facilitating, teaching, kayaking, or engaging in conversation. An awareness of the life inside of me pulses while I live in this world. If I don't, I'm missing my own life. Practicing stillness in this way has grown my capacity for presence. I'm able to sustain presence for a long period of time. I'm able to sit with hard things inside of myself and hard things within other people. I know there is something deeper than the pain, the trauma, the upset. There is something *deeper than that!* I have found it in me, and I am certain it is within you. The greatest gift I offer is being in my own radiance and standing with you to discover yours. I will stand with you while you find your way to your home within.

In Polarity, we cross our ankles and wrists. The joints in the body represent *ether*, which is inner attentiveness, the link between self and source, stillness, longing to remember. I know other traditions say it blocks energy. I find an immediacy to inner attentiveness by doing so. Explore and see what works for you.

I require all of my coaching clients to sit for a minimum of five minutes a day. If we don't find a way to pause and reflect, how are we ever going to make a change? We need to build the skill of observing our mind so we can choose whether soul inspiration or limited beliefs from trauma (be it personal and/or systemic) govern our thinking.

There are many beneficial outcomes of sitting:

- Observing
- Pausing
- Choosing
- Greater clarity
- Inner guidance
- Restoration

In stillness, we are awakened to the awareness of life being in everyone and everything. This attunement reduces harm to ourselves, to each other, and to the world. Being in harmony with the vital current within, in stillness, is the pathway to vibrancy, purpose, and liberation.

Being internally anchored aids us while living in this world. Life experiences are unpredictable: some pleasurable, others painful. Unexpected tragedies can occur. Being tuned in to the center of your being, accessing resources from your vital energy, makes it possible to face such challenges with greater equilibrium. You will have greater balance while facing the world. You'll also conserve your energy within and have access to your inner strength cultivated by stilling the mind.

Yes, Polarity Therapy teaches you how to face the ups and downs of life well.

I recently heard an interview with a woman, who, as a young girl, survived imprisonment in a concentration camp during the time of Hitler. As she was being transported, the girl's mother told her that no one could take her mind away from her. The child took that to heart. She held her own dignity in her mind and saw the Nazi guards as pitiful. They were disconnected from their own humanity, from their own soul knowing. That is how she maintained the will to survive.

INQUIRY: THE SOUL AS THE NORTH STAR

As the mind grows accustomed to pausing, there is space to begin questioning one's thoughts. If we ever hope to reorient, we need to observe and interrogate our mind. Here are some potential questions to ask your mind:

- Does my thought process reflect soul qualities as my guidance? (Soul qualities are unbiased, patient, accepting, neutral, curious, humble, and tolerant.)
- Would I treat other people the way I treat myself?
- What biases might be at play here?
- Is the story I am telling myself confirmation of my own mind stuck in a wounding narrative?
- Am I pausing to determine what is life-giving or what siphons my life energy?
- Am I reacting or reflecting?

The mind develops negative habits of doubt, self-criticism, worry, self-degradation, and unworthiness. Accepting these as normal due to habit and history is not life-giving. It's up to each one of us to use our agency to determine the direction of our attention. We have the power to do so. We are not victims to our mind. We have the soul on our side to inspire and guide us.

One of my friends and colleagues, Sharonda Crome, is fond of saying, "Choose your hard." I live by these words. It *is* hard to make the mind accountable to soul qualities; it's also hard to be driven by negativity, doubt, and judgement. They're both habits of mind, and they're both hard, only one's life-giving and one's not. Which do you want to choose?

Turning our attention inward, helping quiet the mind, allows for the currency of our soul to lead. We experience more vibrancy and equanimity when the soul reigns supreme.

We enliven or sedate. That is up to us.

We have the faculty of discernment. The Latin word for discernment is *discernere*, meaning to sift. Discernment requires insight. It requires the ability to discriminate, to go beyond perception and bias, and obtain a comprehensive picture of any situation. In order for the mind to have access to these skills, pausing and curiosity are required. Tapping into a moral and ethical code connected to soul qualities supports the mind's ability to arrive at a cognitive neutral mind. We, as humans, are differentiated from animals in that we do have these faculties, giving us the agency to make conscious and deliberate moral and ethical choices.

Making life-giving choices becomes an economic approach to sustainable living, where resting and thriving become the new norm. By bringing neutrality to the mind, we strengthen our capacity to humanize everyone across all differences, creating a kinder and more equitable world. By realizing our own true self, we become better human beings.

BIRTHRIGHT

Our birthright is awakening to our radiant soul within.

In our coming home, we know our own worth and value. We join our aliveness. We experience our vitality. Our dignity and our inner safety live in tune with our life force. The current flows at all times, sending and returning over and over again.

Being alive is proof of our deservingness. There is nothing we have to do to earn life itself. We have everything to do with consciously choosing to know our own vital energy.

KINDERGARTEN OF LIFE

Dr. Stone stated that life is a kindergarten from birth until death. The physical world operates in duality, where two opposing poles coexist with a neutral gradient of polarity, spanning both the micro and macro levels. The playing field of experiences exists within these polarities: resistance and flow, pain and pleasure, darkness and light. While we chronologically age and evolve in our consciousness, we don't outgrow this playing field of opposites.

In this playing field, we come up against resistance. The material world is conditioned and limited. Coming up against the restrictions imposed through limitation produces resistance. The resistance is meant as building blocks for the mechanism through which we have the opportunity to learn and grow. As human beings, we have the capacity to make conscious choices. We have the opportunity to evolve our consciousness through the choices we make, be they life-giving or siphoning. We run into difficulty when the mind wants what it wants, not believing there should be conditions or limits. We do not always have the power to change our external experiences. We can learn to utilize resistance for our growth and change instead of becoming stuck.

I've not been able to stop the people I love from dying. We think if we could control our circumstances and experiences, our suffering would be relieved. Suffering occurs in our mind due to expectations and desires not being met. Suffering is meant as a springboard for us to use on our own behalf, to help us learn and grow. Suffering is not meant to be our baseline. The solution is to pause, turn our attention inward, become curious, and choose.

While traveling, I've had plenty of opportunities to work with resistance, suffering, and then choosing. For instance, I've experienced delays and flight cancellations. In 2024, I flew to California to be with a dear friend who was in hospice and near the end of his life. I needed to fly home for three days; then I would return. It was emotional for me leaving, not knowing if he would still be alive when I came back. I had a layover in Dallas on my way home to Cleveland. We arrived in Texas at 4:00 p.m. with an update that the flight to Cleveland was delayed. The time of departure kept changing. A small group of us formed an alliance while waiting, making conjectures about what would happen. Some people yelled at the gate agents, who'd been there since early morning and were required to stay. The employees mostly stayed patient. I felt sorry for them.

At 11:30 p.m., one of the men in our group said he thought they were going to time out and there would be no flight even if the plane did arrive. Sure enough, at midnight, the crew walked off, timing out. Our flight was finally declared cancelled. At this point, I was tired. The line to reach the customer service counter would've been a ninety-minute wait. Frustrated, I got in line, exhausted, upset. I started calculating what time it would be when I would be able to get help. I was tearing up, feeling defeated. I imagined having to sleep on the airport floor. Nighttime was hard for me growing up, not knowing when my father might come into my room. I started imagining how I would be vigilant on the floor, not sleeping, and I panicked. I didn't like the feeling of panicking, so I paused. I realized I was in the future, running the worst-case scenarios instead of realizing I was okay in the moment. I took a breath, reminded myself of resting my spine against a tree, and felt a warm current bathe me from the inside. Then I moved into action.

Everyone was calling the airlines, either being put on hold for hours, or being told there were no flights available for two days. I'm persistent, so I started calling, too. If I was told to wait, I hung up and called again. I did this until someone answered. They found one seat that had just opened up the next morning at 7:00 a.m. They sent me a voucher for a hotel, and off I went for four hours of sleep. The circumstances didn't change; I changed.

Our exploration of this world begins at birth. Babies explore through the senses. They explore movement through stages of development: crawling, walking, running. Young children are fascinated with the world around them, within reach. They play, discover, build, knock things over, draw, fall down, get back up, spill things, and clean them up. There is an innocence and youthfulness in exploring and learning. However, once limits get imposed, or wants are not fulfilled, frustration and unhappiness begin. We lose our youthful innocence and exploration of life.

Think about the relationships you've explored from birth onwards. Family, friends, work, community, neighbors, strangers—at some point, someone disappoints you. People behave in ways you don't want them to. They dislike your ideas. They think they're right and you're wrong. Relationships of any kind have challenges. Resistance. Frustration. Limitation. Disappointment.

When what we want does not match what we experience, where does the fault lie? In the experience or in the mind?

We have preferences for what we like and dislike, what we think is good or bad, right or wrong. When life experiences don't match preferences, we push back against them instead of accepting the limitations and seeing what is possible within them.

Dr. Stone used to say that where there is resistance, there is energy; where there is energy, there is love. By being with the resistance, growth and transformation are possible. Resisting resistance, on the other hand, gets you stuck in it.

PAIN AND PLEASURE

Pain and pleasure are meant as signals, positive and negative poles with a neutral center. Being poles, they have equal value. One is not better than the other. They are experiences that, when held with a neutral mind, are just experiences. However, we tend to either indulge or avoid our pain and pleasure. Either way is out of balance. Looking at pain and pleasure as mechanisms to get our attention changes our relationship to the experience. Touching a hot stove is painful—don't do it again. Someone trying to destroy you or hurt you is a signal to leave. Eating an ice cream cone is pleasurable; eating twenty ice cream cones at a sitting is indulgent. Applying discernment and discrimination to the cues of pain and pleasure helps us determine how to live as stewards of the precious energy of our soul.

If we learned to neglect ourselves in harmful situations (as I did with my dad), it's easy to see how the habit of indulging in pain might seem normal and familiar. People stay in harmful relationships because, historically, they don't know there is a choice.

People deny themselves positive feelings and/or indulge in positive feelings. We're creatures of habit, and we want to learn and grow out of habits that limit vibrancy and liberation. We need to bring a curious mind to our resistance so we can observe, choose, and learn. Having access to the life energy within brings a youthful vitality to learning. Nothing is meant to be perfect or to go our way all the time. The mind revolts when the conditions of the world place limitations. That's just the way of life. We're more than our experiences. We're a living energy connected to the source of life.

ATTRACTION AND REPULSION

Magnetic forces are at play in this kindergarten of life.

Attraction and repulsion are natural forces. They coordinate with whatever the positive pole is. When the soul is governing as the positive pole, we attract positive, life-giving thoughts. We attract foods that nourish us. We attract people who support our deepest self. We repel negative, self-defeating thoughts. We repel foods that dull our vibrancy. We repel people who don't have our best interest at heart. Bringing the mind toward neutrality allows the natural forces of attraction and repulsion to work on our behalf.

When the mind assumes the positive pole, the forces of attraction and repulsion are at play. If lack of worthiness is the positive pole, then attracting foods, ideas and people will reinforce the lack of worthiness. In tandem, what is life-giving ends up being repelled. Scary, right?

DETERMINING YOUR NORTH STAR IS CRUCIAL

Repulsion is natural and just exists. The mind judges. Judging is not natural or life-giving. Judging creates divisiveness. Judging others people. And it has a charge to it.

Repulsion is a force operating with a neutral gradient. It can't help but do what it does. The mind, on the other hand, has choice. It's important to be able to discern what force is at play inside of ourselves. I'm personally repulsed by horror movies. That doesn't make horror movies bad or people that watch them bad. If I become judgmental about what repels me, I can produce harm. For example, I might be uncomfortable with someone from a different culture whose rituals repel me. However, if I become judgmental about their practices, I could become verbally insulting, dismiss their tradition, or act out my judgement in some way.

As we live, our experiences are the building blocks for our learning. How we relate to them and how we learn from them is up to us. We have the power to choose how we respond to experiences, to ourselves, and to people. We have the opportunity to apply soul qualities to our experiences. We have the power to choose whether we build a positive charge and behave in a way that is life-giving or fracture our connection to life, fracturing our connection to ourselves and ultimately to each other in the process.

REST AS THE BASELINE FOR TRULY LIVING

In the context of Polarity, rest means neutrality, impartiality, equanimity, stillness, deep listening, and knowing. Think of this as stillness at the center of our being. It's our birthright to access the stillness within us as our baseline for being as we learn and grow. We do so by attending to the internal hearth fire within. Being resourced by the vital energy is found in rest. Then there is an inherent knowing of belonging, value, safety, and love within.

This precious currency radiates freely inside you twenty-four hours a day, seven days a week. It is the supplier of energy that lets your heart beat, lets you know love and your true worth. However, in our society, we equate rest with being exhausted, depleted. We wait too long to be restored. Energy is squandered through over expenditure and seeking your value, worth in the material world of form.

I promise you, it's possible to rest inside while being active. Rest occurs in stillness and aliveness. At seventy-two, I'm very active while resting. I don't want to miss the currency of life within me while in action. Hike with me some time. There is great stillness in me while I have a quick and steady pace. Consider rest as your baseline. See what more is possible for you to live vibrantly.

Reversing the mind from positive to neutral is the lifelong path of Polarity. It requires dedication and focus. The reward is becoming aware of the radiance of that which gives you your very life—your soul. If you accept that life is a kindergarten from birth until death, and you know you'll experience limitations and resistance, doesn't that compel you to search for the "deeper than that?" Life must be about more than just resistance.

Renowned sociologist and author Laurel Richardson is a dear friend of mind. Though she is technically my ex-mother-in-law, she still feels like family. When she got COVID at eighty-six years old, she fell down the steep stairs in her home from the second to the first floor. It's unclear how long she lay at the bottom of the stairs.

Two months prior to the fall, I'd sat down with my husband and shared with him that I had a strong calling to help Laurel with care. I was thinking about end-of-life care. We live two hours away from Laurel, and I wanted to know if he would be supportive. He agreed. I visited Laurel in Columbus and shared my thoughts with her. She was touched and relieved: She knew the strength of my caregiving from watching me with my mother.

None of us knew the caregiving would happen two months later, but I kept my word.

Laurel ended up in the trauma one hospital with two cervical and three thoracic spine fractures. She had broken ribs, a broken wrist that required surgery, and a contusion on her head the size of a grapefruit resulting in a concussion. She was in a neck and thoracic back brace that required her to lay flat for two weeks until they determined she would not need spinal surgery. She was heavily drugged with Fentanyl at first, which resulted in horrible hallucinations. (Eventually her son had the medication changed.) Everything was hard and seemed hopeless to her. I was going down every week for a few days at a time. I stayed in daily contact with her. Three weeks in, I got a call that she was going to the ICU; they said she had a stroke. Something about this did not feel right to me, so I rushed to the hospital, arriving before they took her.

I went into the room, and she responded to me immediately. She told me she didn't want wood for food anymore. I understood what Laurel meant. Wood was a metaphor for horrible food. There was an amazing patient assistant in the room who'd grown fond of Laurel. I asked her if they would stop feeding Laurel wood. She agreed. The other staff thought she was mentally off from a stroke. I kept talking to Laurel, orienting her to familiar things, and she became coherent. The nursing staff came into the room to evaluate her again and saw her recovery. Soon they realized it was hospital delirium, disorientation from staring at beige ceiling tiles for weeks on end, not knowing day from night or having external stimulation.

Laurel was moved to the brain and spine hospital. Gradually she was allowed to sit up and increase motion. She shared with me she wanted this to be over. She didn't want to live. She felt overwhelmed at any advancement, feeling that it was impossible for her. Her mind was in a groove of defeat, despondence, and hopelessness. It was understandable. She'd ask me to put my hands on her to see if her soul was leaving her body. I have the skill of feeling the life energy in the body, the pulsing from pole to pole. I have sat with many people dying, experiencing the soul's current leaving the body. I know the difference. When I put my hands on Laurel, in spite of all her injuries, there was a strong pulse from pole to pole. Her soul was vibrant in her body. I shared that with her.

"Your soul has more in store for you," I said.

Laurel wanted to feel what I was experiencing. We tried different practices. I did nervous system energy work with her (hands-on) until she could rest inside and experience the well-spring of life in inner stillness. She discovered it. It was beautiful beyond words to witness. We did this over and over again because her negative mind would take over.

And yet, at one point, she decided it was all too much again. She called a family meeting with a palliative care, end-of-life doctor. I arrived before anyone else. I called a friend to support me in staying neutral while sharing my thoughts in a way that was open-ended. I asked her if I could share my perspective. She said yes. I shared that I believe dying has a divine time, that her situation was not terminal. I wondered without assisted suicide how she might accomplish this. Starving to death? She looked at me, paused, and had some lightbulb go off inside of her. When the doctor and family did arrive, she asked different questions about her recovery. Would she walk again? Would she go home? No one had ever sat with her and given her the prognosis. They said she would walk again with rehab and that she would eventually be able to go home. Her spirit became uplifted. What her soul was asking of her she now joined.

Laurel did recover. She's now walking. She sold her home after a year and moved into a beautiful apartment for people fifty-five and older. She is more at peace and happier than she ever has been in her life. She tells me that she's grateful to me and that if it weren't for my intervention, she'd be dead. Her mind needed to adjust to what her soul was calling for. I am so honored to have been guided to be part of the process and her acceptance in the process.

Fighting the soul with the mind or joining the soul with the mind is our choice point. Laurel was valiant in her choice. Though she had not investigated the depth of her soul, her story illustrates that it's never too late.

This is a prime example of the value of tuning in to the vital life energy within. There's knowledge and wisdom beyond what our mind can conjure. Training the mind to be neutral and receptive to the guidance of the soul gives great purpose and direction for our life. Reversing the polarity of the mind from the positive pole to the neutral gradient supports us knowing and experiencing our inner radiance. This spiritual bank account goes with us upon our death.

To watch a teaching video of The Path of Polarity, go to https://youtu.be/vb6iefiW_Eg.

CHAPTER 11

LONGING VS. WOUNDING—KNOW THE DIFFERENCE

LONGING

Longing is directional and purposeful; it's a yearning ache for deeper contact with your true self. Longing is associated with the incoming current of the wireless system. When you join longing with introspection, you return to and remember your inner radiance. Longing isn't associated with an experience, a person, or a situation. It's an absence that nothing in this world will alleviate. And yet, if you let it, longing may serve as a generative impulse.

Choosing your longing requires:

1. An understanding and inner acknowledgement that nothing in this world will ultimately fulfill and sustain you. You associate the hunger you have inside for remembering and returning to your vital life force— your soul. Your soul current is pulsing inside as your inner treasure.

2. You come to recognize the yearning, aching, and burning inside of you as a gift rather than thinking there is something wrong with you.

3. The yearning helps you slow down the impulse of seeking in the outer world of form, turning your attention inward. You join the natural impulse and direction of longing for your homecoming.

4. You use your discernment to distinguish the sensation of longing as life-giving rather than painful. It's not associated with past trauma or wounds. It's vital to uncouple longing from trauma—otherwise, you will associate your longing with danger. You'll ignore the signal of your hunger for your own salvation. Instead, you'll reify your trauma, bonding with the narrative and stories that spawned from it. When your trauma narratives become your North Star rather than your longing, you miss the opportunity to be fed by the eternal, life-giving source inside of you.

Are you looking for the solution to your restlessness and unease in the constantly changing world of form? Or are you making longing your partner, allowing it to compel you toward the nourishment and fulfillment you seek inside of you?

While teaching, I share that longing is a natural and necessary component of our human experience. It's an inner aching not associated with any circumstance or life event. At some point, there is a growing awareness that the comfort one seeks is not available in the material world. As we sense this world is not our true home, a homesickness arises for something deeper. Many of my students have shared that having this knowledge as a young child would've been helpful. Without context for this type of ache, they interpreted it as something wrong with them.

Personally, I welcome the ache of longing. When the hunger lessens, I feel lost. The ache, the yearning, impels me to seek within. It helps me to remember and return to the great gift of life inside me, where my soul calls me home.

Longing leads us to love. As Dr. Stone writes in *Polarity Therapy*, Volume 1, Book 3, "Love itself is an attraction in one direction—towards its center." I distinguish between personal love, which has a personal agenda of attachments and expectations, and non-personal love, which exists beyond the personality and without an agenda. Non-personal love is the energy of the soul current, sending and reverberating inside of you at the center of your being. The sending of this love is unbiased and unending.

Just like the battery, the sending of this primary soul current must return. The love that's sending through you must return through magnetism. The current is attracted in one direction; the outgoing current becomes the incoming current, back to the center of giving. Love begets love. You see, by returning to and remembering consciously who we truly are, longing leads us to love.

I find great comfort and relief in this. I've always longed for the mystery, the "deeper than that." The system works on my behalf, intelligently, purposefully, and directionally. It's my job to choose to join its function. Knowing what it offers motivates me to focus my attention on behalf of my longing. It's a much better option for me than being stuck in my mind hating myself and wanting to die as a result of my wounding.

WOUNDING

Wounding occurs when there is an impact to the body, emotion, and/or character. Most of us have experienced wounding in all three categories. With the impact from an incoming blow, whether it be physical, mental, or emotional, a startled, adrenalized response occurs. Without recovering from the startle, people find themselves habituated with a fight-or-flight response as their baseline of being. This is how a person becomes distant to their rest, inner stillness, and restoration.

Most of us know pain is associated with wounding. Physical injuries from wounds are easy to address through practical solutions and medical expertise. Clean the wound, apply ointment, get stitches if necessary, change bandages, and continue treatment until healing is complete. The body's own vital energy is a resource for healing. A scar may remain, but living will resume over time.

Emotional, mental, and character wounding is harder to address. Now the psyche is involved. Early trauma often gets buried, unavailable to the conscious mind. In an early trauma, the person harmed blames themselves—usually there's insufficient neurological development to think differently. Of course, this can also occur with harm at any point in life. Rape victims often blame themselves.

In this state, shame, self-deprecation, unworthiness, unlovability, and self-hatred arise. These thoughts take on a life of their own, abandoning the wisdom and inherent knowledge inside of you. The thoughts dominate, becoming the point of reference for all future events. Wounding begets wounding.

I experienced this when a dear friend of mine brought closure to our relationship. The approach was dignified and honest. The friend shared the undeniability of our love, yet they felt a need to end the relationship. At the time, they didn't have an explanation. Clean and clear. Painful, yes. Unexpected, yes. Without a beat, I routed the information through my childhood wound narrative. I spiraled down a dark tunnel. Pounding, self-deprecating voices yelled at me, telling me how bad I was, how unlovable I was. The wound of the past got activated before I could pause, take a breath, or even feel sad. I was suffering.

Having been down this road before, I knew I needed to recover from a trigger. I used the same tools I've used to restore myself many times before. I reminded myself that while this was unwanted and unexpected, I was not being raped while family members watched, no one coming to my aid. Now I had trusted friends who I could call, friends who would support me, who cared about me. I reminded myself that I'm a radiant soul, part and parcel of the source of life for all of creation. I rested against my spine where my soul pulses inside of me. I lay on the ground harmonizing with nature. I didn't try to get rid of the self-hatred—I knew well enough from experience that it would only dig its heels in deeper. Instead, I let it be there, reminding myself with compassion that the negative emotion was (misguidedly) trying to protect me. "Fuck the shame," one of my dear friends said, and that made me laugh so hard, it took me out of my suffering. The space created allowed me to continue to help myself.

This is the path of Polarity for me. Pause, create space, give the mind another positive pole to refer to. It took a few days to really regain my equanimity. A few days rather than years—what a welcome change!

I read this chapter to Laurel while visiting her in rehab. An immediate response arose from within her. She summed it up by stating that longing is an ache, expansive, full of light, and purposeful, unlike wounding, which she finds constrictive and dark.

Having your own way of knowing the difference helps you choose. Remember: Wounding signals danger. Longing signals remembering and returning. It's important to uncouple any association with the ache of longing from danger. Instead, see longing as a gift to serve you. Your longing will guide you to the positive pole of your soul, where you're welcomed home.

CHAPTER 12

STILLNESS VS. SEDATION (AND HOW TO KNOW THE DIFFERENCE)

"The soul has been given its own ears to hear things the mind does not understand."

—Rumi

STILLNESS

Stillness at the center of our being is a treasure house of resources. In stillness, the positive virtues of the soul reign supreme. It's here that the true self is discovered, underneath the mental chatter, pain and pleasure, light and darkness. In the center of stillness is freedom. Many religions, philosophers, and poets write about the power of stillness. As T.S. Eliot writes in his poem, "Wait Without Hope," "I said to my soul, be still, and wait without hope . . . So the darkness shall be the light, and the stillness the dancing."

Cultivating stillness requires turning the attention inward, where the eternal storehouse of truth and love resides. Stillness is attuning to the power of the soul pulsing inside of you. Stillness is very alive, vibrant. Stillness includes all, the totality of the soul's radiance, which is but a drop from the source of life. Stillness requires focused attention. The practice of sitting in stillness requires staying with any thoughts, feelings, or sensations that arise. Over time, trust and faith grow. By staying with what arises, you are more than these thoughts, feelings, and sensations. You become aware that you are held by the well of life inside. Leaning on the resource within gives you support and confidence to face whatever you have to go through in this life. We can't control our external circumstances. Why not face life with this great inner resource?

Stillness provides great benefits for your life:

- Still waters run deep. Underneath the surface of chaos from the external world, there is a **refuge** inside your own stillness.
- The treasure of your **deepest self** is found in stillness.
- **Clarity** from a turbulent mind is found in stillness.
- Learning to **surrender** is found in stillness.
- **Humility** is in stillness.
- **Inner knowing** resides in stillness.
- **Authenticity** emerges from stillness.
- **Inner strength** deepens in stillness.
- **Rest and restoration** exist at your center.

When I was young, I found refuge in stillness through my heroines of Grace, Mercy, and Love. While my father raped me, I accessed complete quiet, blocking what was happening to my body. I was held in sacredness, on another level of being. In my closet, too, while my body was in a fetal position, I found inner stillness and freedom. Stillness became the only way to know safety or grace inside of me.

Longing guided me to seek stillness. I found refuge in stillness—I still do. Longing is the inward pull that brings you to the gift of stillness. How do you seek stillness in yourself?

SEDATION

Sitting in stillness can be challenging. We have to face ourselves in stillness. There is nowhere to run or hide. You with yourself. Some days it's just plain daunting.

Sedation seems easier, providing a temporary distraction from any pain, hurt, or discomfort. The reflex to self-numb is automatic, protective, and avoidant. We devise many creative ways of sedating: overeating, undereating, overindulging in alcohol and/or mind-altering substances, exorbitant shopping, binge watching TV, excessive exercise, and more. The discomfort, hurt, and pain are still there. Without providing the gift of inner resource to the hurt, an emptiness can arise. Back on the sedation train to avoid the emptiness. It goes on and on and on. Sedation leads to sedation. Sedation seems like stillness. We can pretend we are still when we are actually sedating feelings, sensations, and even our own knowing.

Stillness leads you to resource and aliveness. Yes, sensations and feelings might arise. These sensations and feelings are temporary, though sometimes it doesn't seem that way. Intense feelings can be overwhelming, but they don't last forever. With an anchor in stillness, you can offer the intensity a depth of resource. Without that anchor, sedation leaves you under-resourced.

Having access to feeling and sensations gives you information to make decisions about how to take care of yourself: setting boundaries, creating meaningful and life-giving work, challenging the mind. If you feel yourself, you will be able to take better care of yourself. If you are numb, there are no cues to lead you to self-care.

And yet there are times when making a conscious choice to sedate is a good idea.

Eight years ago, I was in the dentist chair having a procedure that required me keeping my mouth open for a long period of time. I was lying on my back with a male dentist's hands in my mouth. (Even as I'm writing, I have to breathe and stay in the present moment, to not have my history warn me of danger.)

Toward the end of the procedure, the dentist took an impression of my upper teeth. He was having a difficult time removing the mold. He kept tugging down on it, trying to take it off. The mold wouldn't budge—he began sweating. Concern flashed in his eyes. That made *me* nervous. This went on for a long time before he realized he would have to saw the mold off. Lying on my back, him above me, helpless, my body started to have a memory. I could feel it coming on, but I couldn't talk with the contraption in my mouth. I started to feel overwhelmed. I wanted to scream "LET ME UP!" Tears ran down my face. At that moment, I decided to numb—I knew that was the smartest thing for me to do. Having a full-blown memory in the chair right then and there did not seem like a good idea. It still took some time to get the mold off, and when the dentist was done, I sat up, gasping for air. I blurted to the dental assistant I was having a body memory from a childhood rape.

The dental assistant looked at me with compassion. Then, she asked if it was okay if she held me. I consented. She sat in the dentist chair next to me and put her arms around me. The feelings came pouring out. I sobbed.

We always have choice. Choosing consciously allows us to use our neutral mind to determine our thoughts, actions, and behavior. Neither choice is right or wrong. If you choose to consciously sedate, you interrupt doing it habitually, reflexively. You might think to yourself, in your own version of that dentist's chair, "Right now, I want to numb." You'd be acknowledging what numbing does and doesn't afford you. You'd be choosing to numb consciously, thus allowing you to un-numb and feel when it's safe to do so. Then you'd have the freedom to return to stillness consciously as well.

CHAPTER 13

ALONENESS VS. ISOLATION (KNOW THE DIFFERENCE)

Aloneness and relationality naturally belong together. Your soul enters into the material world alone at birth, and ultimately leaves the material world at the time of death. While other people might be there to witness these acts, your soul comes and goes on its own behalf. While your soul is in your body living the life you have now, there is an illusion of individuality and separateness. However, the soul is inherently interconnected to the source of life for all of creation, part of an energy web beyond our cognitive understanding.

Aloneness and interrelatedness are intertwined. Life begets life.

There are times when being alone with yourself is generative, restful, and nourishing. This is when part of your attention is aware of the vital energy inside of you and/or you are aware of the interconnectedness of all of life.

For me, the primary way I luxuriate and get restored while being alone is in and with nature. Hiking, kayaking, walking, laying on the earth, witnessing a sunset, or simply smelling a flower by myself brings me great joy. I live near a National Park and many city parks that provide hours and hours of hiking. I explore as many of them as possible. While hiking alone, I find myself all of a sudden smiling from ear to ear. The sheer delight of taking one step after another, smelling the dirt, feeling the different textures under my hiking shoes, listening to the birds, and feeling the breeze makes me so happy. I am part of something alive. I also cherish finding a spot to sit and be. In the quiet, I hear the bounty of sounds the natural world offers.

However, aloneness is not always experienced as being nourishing and restoring. When aloneness is no longer intertwined with interrelatedness, being alone can feel lonely, unsafe, devastating, and even dangerous. A young child's mind doesn't have the neurological function to differentiate; it blames itself for fractures to connection. In adulthood, experiences are still routed through this self-blaming perception, leading to pervasive feelings of rejection and abandonment (whether rejection or abandonment is occurring or not). The perception becomes personal when others do not witness, affirm, support, and validate you. This creates a sense of rejection and abandonment. Aloneness, then, becomes about separation instead of interconnectedness. Until the natural intertwinement of aloneness and relationality is restored, further social interactions get routed through the lenses of separateness, abandonment, and/or rejection.

There is a great cost to operating with the belief you are separate, isolated, and without the resource of interconnectedness. Suffering and feeling removed become perceptual habits until a yearning for something "deeper than that" reunites you with your own soul currency. Your vital life force is there even when people have betrayed you. You do not have to be limited by your experiences. There is a pathway to resource and aliveness you deserve.

ISOLATION

Isolation results from a disconnection to interpersonal relationships and the outside world. Social isolation can be characterized by having few or no relationships with other people, very little social contact, and a lack of support from others. Loneliness, on the other hand, is marked by distress due to a gap between the desire for social connection and actual experiences.

The impact of isolation is far-reaching. Take leadership, for example. People who are leaders have often unwittingly organized their lives around isolation and lack of support that will take them to the point of exhaustion. They'll put in long hours and take on more responsibility than what's required of them. This leads to burnout. Their thought process is that they have to do *everything* themselves. They know they'll get it done the way they want it done.

When I coach these leaders, I ask them to identify the costs of that mindset. I also ask if that's the outcome they want for themselves. The answer is almost always no. Then I ask what they do want for themselves. It's crucial to come to the awareness that the cost of leading from isolation is too high. When these individuals can identify that they want to lead differently, we devise a strategic plan to make the shift. Soon they're able to find ways to lead while also being supported. They even make time for self-care. They shift their leadership from a place of overwhelm and burn out to one of being supported and rested, and guess what? They're still productive!

Living with personal isolation reinforces the mindset that you lack resources or that you're somehow deficient. Usually there is a belief of unworthiness associated with being connected to or supported by others. Loneliness ensues. Sometimes people are so used to loneliness, they just accept it. Yet our inherent wireless system is interconnected. The hope is that some inner impulse guides the person to restoration and healing to choose to be in relationship more, even if it's with just a few people.

I had to learn to overcome isolation to create a trusted community. From a very young age, I trained myself to hide in an encapsulated space where I believed no one could hurt or reach me. I wanted to be invisible—after all, visibility was patently unsafe for me. While physically in a room with other people, internally I was tucked away in a dark cavern. Withdrawing in this way, I protected myself through inner isolation. In the process, though, I cut myself off from the deeper part of me and from others.

While it was a good idea when I was in my childhood home, this internal isolation endured past the point when I actually really needed it. Trust was never easy for me. After all, I had been betrayed at such a young age.

Eventually, I got tired of my imprisonment. It was limiting my choices and impacting my loneliness. I had to find a way to stop hiding; I had to climb out of my cavern. I had to learn to become available for connection and support.

I used the wireless system to retrain my mind to see the truth of interconnectedness, to learn that I deserved support and connection to myself and others. With the support and guidance of trusted therapists and great friends, I found my way home to aloneness and interrelatedness. While it was a lot of work, it was worthy work.

Learning the difference gives you the choice to determine what is best for you. How do you know the difference between restorative aloneness or isolating aloneness, aloneness that alienates you from your deepest self? Which of the following statements resonates with you?

> I **alone** choose to seek my vibrancy from within, to seek my value and knowing within. In my aloneness, I have the opportunity to access the vital current pulsing inside of me to know myself more deeply. I alone listen to what is being asked of me from deep inside.

OR

> I **alone** choose to see the world through a lens of rejection, abandonment, isolation, and separateness. Being alone from this perspective becomes hard, scary, sad, protective, and defensive. Every experience is routed through this lens.

As you learn to distinguish between aloneness and isolation, these questions will help you gain more agency in your choices and more awareness of your mindset and habits:

- What are ways you luxuriate being alone?
- Do you recognize your loneliness as a gap between what you desire interpersonally and what you are experiencing?
- When lonely, do you sedate or turn inward to follow your longing?
- How do you isolate from yourself? From others?

- How do you restore yourself?

SUMMARY

As a human being, you have the opportunity in this life to remember the truth of who you are, a radiant soul.

You have a wireless operating system designed for your remembering. Your soul is the positive pole; the body (material world) is the negative pole; and the mind is the neutral gradient. Your soul sends and returns to itself over and over again. The soul guides and inspires your mind. Then the power of your soul is able to be contacted directly without any interference.

However, this is a world of duality, of polarities. There has to be light and dark. You need to forget in order to remember. Forgetting happens when your mind takes over and assumes the positive pole. Distance gets created from your own source of wisdom and knowing from your soul.

It is up to you to choose consciously if you want to know the truth of who you are at the center of your being. In order to do so, you are required to reverse your mind from thinking it's the positive pole to neutrality to restore the ideal order.

Longing is your gift.

Remembering is your birthright.

You are the steward of your precious life energy, given to you by the source of life for all of creation.

My wish for you is that there's a hunger inside of you that compels you to find the "deeper than that" inside of you. You are already worthy; it's the truth of who you are.

PART III

EVERYONE:
LIFE UNITES
US ALL

CHAPTER 14

LIFE UNITES US ALL

THE TRUTH OF LIFE ENERGY

The source of life energy enlivens all of creation, creating an interconnected web. Energy is in everyone and everything.

There's a primary energy source that is the positive pole for all of creation. The source sends with a magnificent outpouring of eternal love generously, unlimited, unbiased. The source sends without discrimination, without hierarchy of value, and without divisions; it unites all of life in a myriad of expressions. Whether in rocks, plants, bodies of water, human beings, or planetary forces, life energy exists throughout the material world. We're all interconnected through the benevolent gift of life.

As human beings, we have the opportunity in this life to consciously tune in to the current of this emanating energy, our soul, within our own body. By aligning with this vital energy at the center of our being, we awaken not only to the true awareness of who we are but also to the living interconnected web of life.

In this way, we become stewards of our own precious life, while also becoming stewards for all of life: the planet, animals, forests, rivers, and oceans. By deepening our care for life within and without, we'll naturally evolve to become better human beings. We'll generate positive energy while reducing harmful impact. We'll come into greater harmony within ourselves and with the outer world. We'll become increasingly sensitive to our impact: What hurts me hurts you; what hurts you hurts me. We'll experience greater waves of peace flowing through us, greater equanimity, and greater resource to face life's challenges.

An etheric sonic core links our essential self to the source, an eternal ocean of love. We have access to our soul pulsing pole to pole, reverberating inside of us. We are designed through the wireless operating system to realize and remember who we truly are. We're fully equipped to know our treasure within.

In the system of Polarity, where life energy is in everyone and everything, each person deserves to be fully alive and unapologetically radiant. Everyone deserves to live with a vibrant sense of well-being, freedom, equanimity, resource, and rest.

Polarity provides us with a transformative relationship with rest by moving beyond survival-driven reactivity to being restored through the power of soul currency within. Resting soon becomes a baseline for being. Learning how to take action while resting becomes the norm. Resting is no longer allocated to exhaustion, as an action of recovery. Instead, it becomes the economic resource for vibrant living, purpose, and liberation.

SOCIAL BEINGS

As part of an interconnected web of life, we are naturally social beings. We flourish by relying on interactions with others and creating social bonds. Human connections support not only our survival but our consequent thriving.

If we, as social creatures, created our connections and our bonds with the knowledge of life in everyone and everything, our communities and social systems would reflect the value of every life. Our laws, policies, and neighborhoods would reflect the true nature of life itself. Access to resources and opportunities, education and health care, would be equitable. While this world will never be perfect, we can aspire to come together as social creatures honoring life in everyone and everything. Collectively we strive to honor the sacredness of life, to live united and serve the whole of life together.

FORESTS AS LIVING EXAMPLES

Forests demonstrate how the web of life works to support life thriving. Forests naturally thrive due to complex diversity, communication, and natural interdependence.

Diversity of plant life protects the forest from complete devastation when there are outside threats to survival. For example, if a forest is planted by humans with only one variety of tree, that grove of trees runs the risk of total devastation. The arrival of an insect carrying a lethal disease that destroys that variety leaves the forest completely wiped out. Without a diverse root system remaining, soil erosion emerges, and the costs run deep. The land impacted threatens our food security. Rivers and oceans weaken. Not having complex diversity is costly.

Trees know how to communicate and care for the good of the whole. They have a way to signal threats and diseases. In a forest, trees develop an interdependent root system that reaches deep and wide. The strongest roots provide nourishment to the weaker roots. The interlocking roots provide strength and support during a heavy windstorm. The root system has the capacity to store food. The larger the root system, the greater the support for the canopy and for collective thriving.

I am fortunate to live surrounded by trees and rich biodiversity, so I get to witness the power of nature. I learn firsthand by observing. I'm routinely amazed at how few trees get uprooted in heavy winds. As I walk among the abundant diversity of trees teeming with life, I see some trees' roots are more above the ground before disappearing below the surface; other trees' roots go directly underground. I see trees reaching for the sun, coming to a shared canopy. Roots below, canopy above.

As I learn about nature—or, as I learn from nature—I wonder how we as social creatures can mimic the intelligence found in forests. What do you imagine is possible to learn from diverse forests, living networks that communicate and thrive through interdependence?

CHAPTER 15

MY INNER KNOWING INCONGRUENT WITH SOCIAL DISPARITIES

believe at some point in our lives, we've all had the experience of unity or oneness. A mesmerizing sunset. The sound of purple martins on their migratory path. When separateness disappears with a hug. Walking in the forest, sitting by a waterfall, sledding in fresh snow. A sense of unity between two energies, like that between the self and the universe. In unity, separation dissolves. In the context of Polarity, unity and oneness arrive when the mind is neutral between the poles of the soul and the material body. Then the awareness of interconnectedness between self and the universe and all of life automatically arises.

From an early age, I've known about the unity of life, and for this I am forever grateful. Finding solace in my heroines of Mercy, Grace, and Love during my rape gave me access to this knowing. As I was held by my heroines, I experienced a sense of unity, awe, and the eternal. In the utter stillness, only oneness existed. Horrible things were happening to my body, my heart, and my mind, but my spirit was, and is, whole and holy. That's what I knew. My knowing was non-cognitive yet fully aware.

The beauty of discovering eternal love while surviving became the foundation for my superpowers later in life. My capacity to access the interconnectedness of all of life has served me in becoming vibrant, reducing harm, and embodying the value of unity while coaching and teaching.

The holy state of oneness was in stark contrast to what I was witnessing everywhere I looked. There was a chasm between my inner knowing and what I was witnessing. Obviously my home environment did not reflect care and interconnectedness. My father found a way to numb himself to the reality that I was his precious daughter; he used me for his own needs and did so for many years. He didn't value my life. His actions confused me. How could I understand the harm I was experiencing when he was supposed to love and protect me? Love and abuse got linked together. Love no longer had the association of holiness and oneness.

The chasm made me begin to doubt my internal knowing of union, of oneness. It was the beginning of separating my inner-knowing from what I experienced outside of me. I diminished my own truth.

While teaching and working with clients, I've discovered that almost everyone I have worked with has diminished their inner knowing. When the world does not operate from the foundational truth of interconnectedness and unity, reflections of separateness, harm, and fractures ensue. Guiding people to reclaim their inherent knowing is so rewarding.

Growing up, I also witnessed class, racial, religious, and gender disparities. What I saw and experienced created a chasm in me, estranging me from my inner knowing. These experiences brought me face-to-face with how our social systems, designed through the false reality of separateness and individualism, are driving forces that distance us from our deepest selves.

Through Polarity principles and practices, I began to attune to my life energy and became restored to my deepest knowing. I've found ways to interrupt my mind's biases, which once shaped my preferences to embrace similarities while excluding certain differences. As I evolved through Polarity, I changed how I coach. Today I require all of my coaching clients to unpack the ways they have been socialized around class, race, gender, and religion. I don't believe we can truly be our deepest selves unless we understand the superficial and unconscious ways we have internalized separateness, divisiveness, and unjust hierarchies.

MY WITNESSING: THE CHASM BEGINS

I grew up in Bexley, Ohio, in an upper-middle class neighborhood. My parents were both doctors: my father a psychiatrist, my mother just short of taking her residency in psychiatry. We belonged to a country club and lived a very comfortable life. We always had a domestic worker to take care of the house and make dinners for our family.

My father was a tyrant that everyone in my family was afraid of. But Mary, our domestic worker, was not afraid of him. Mary was my favorite person who worked for us prior to my parents' divorce (when I was eleven). A woman of deep faith, Mary's children were grown, and she often shared how much she loved being with us as she did not have grandchildren and missed the stages of young children. My brother Ralph and I were pretty much inseparable—I was five and he was six when Mary was there. She was a ray of sunshine and reprieve from the haunts of my father's abuse. Ralph and I spent a lot of time with Mary. She wore an apron that she pretended was magic. She would tell us a story, have us close our eyes, and then a piece of candy would appear from the apron. We were always delighted, filled with wonder and joy.

One day, Mary was in the kitchen making dinner. My dad came home, which always produced a cloud of dread, sucking Mary's warmth from the atmosphere. My dad was smoking a cigar that reeked throughout the whole downstairs. I trailed behind him as he walked into the kitchen, cigar smoke filling the air.

Mary spoke up. She asked my father to either put out the cigar or smoke it in another room as it was interfering with her cooking.

I remember freezing, staring. How did she have such courage?

My father didn't like her courage. He didn't like anyone questioning him or denying him, certainly not her. He told her in an aggressive, hostile tone—a tone that scared me—to leave and never come back. I watched her take off her magic apron and walk out of the kitchen. As she passed by me, she touched my shoulder and told me she was sorry, but she had to go.

I was heartbroken. I didn't comprehend the forces at play here. I didn't understand what I now do: that I was witnessing a Black woman of a lower-class speak up to a white man, my father, her employer. The goodness in Mary—her love, her connectivity, her imagination—was not valued. My attention got alerted. This is how things can work.

My neighborhood consisted of white families. The Black people I saw were limited to domestic workers, janitorial support, or kitchen staff in the school. Where we lived, the deeds on the houses excluded Black people from purchasing homes. When I was in second grade, the first Black family moved into an apartment above the local drugstore. Maybe because of my experience with Mary, I didn't think twice about playing with the Black girl that was in my grade. I went to her apartment, met her mother, and enjoyed my play time. We played with dolls, told stories, and had a snack.

I went home happy. But after dinner that night, my mother received a phone call. Someone was informing her of my actions; the caller told my mom she should forbid me to play with this child. My mother explained to me what happened. I don't remember what she said to the person that called, nor do I remember exactly what she said to me. What I do recall is her sadness while reporting this. She didn't explicitly forbid me to play with the girl, but she sounded concerned about me. How could I understand her sadness? It was all very confusing. I didn't play with the girl again, and within a few weeks of our playdate, the family disappeared.

My innocence led me to play with her. My inner knowing signaled safety to me. And yet I couldn't forget the call my mom had received, which signaled danger when I didn't feel danger or experience any kind of threat or harm. That signaling made me question my own knowledge and experience. Was I supposed to see this family as dangerous? Inside, I had a gut feeling it was about race but no cognitive understanding. The chasm kept widening. My inner knowing was up against racial disparity.

A few years after this experience, my parents got divorced. The day my mother learned my father was leaving, she cried hysterically and looked both defeated and relieved. My father had been tormenting us for as long as I can remember. He used to belittle my mom in front of us. He would sit us all down in the living room and demean her, sometimes kick her in the shin. When he was finished, I lay there on the couch, curled up in a ball, immobilized. My mom would eventually take me upstairs and give me something to medicate me.

I didn't really understand it when my mother told me that my father was leaving and had spoken to an attorney. I was in fourth grade, and I was the first person I knew whose family was experiencing a divorce. Trying to understand what a divorce entailed, I asked my teacher what exactly a "fraternity" was. She explained to me that it was an organization for men, and I did not understand why my mom would be so upset over that. After dinner, talking with my mother in her distress, I realized there's a real difference between a divorce attorney and a fraternity. I suppose it's hard for a marriage to end even when it is destructive. The unknown is terrifying. The known is exactly that: known.

My father got a really good attorney; my mother did not. She didn't have much fight left in her after having been beaten down for a long time. She did get the house in the divorce agreement, but only $6,000 a year for her and us four kids. She decided to go back and do her residency and received another $6,000 a year for her training. We lived off $12,000 a year, a very different income than what we were used to with my father's earnings. While we stayed in the big house, we were living a very different economic reality than my friends. I started making my own clothes and babysitting to earn money. We drank powdered milk and ate instant mashed potatoes. My friends all went shopping for the latest styles of clothes and shoes, something I could no longer afford to do. I remember wanting a certain Villager brand dress so badly that I bought a pattern and some material with my babysitting money and made one that matched everyone else's style. No one knew that I'd made it myself. I still have that dress.

While no one sat me down and told me that I was less valuable with more limited economic resources than before, I sure felt that way. While I was being resilient and creative, I also felt so much shame and unworthiness. Now I wonder: Where did these thoughts and feelings come from if they weren't said to me explicitly? The forces of social systems became a collective North Star in my mind without my awareness. When a collective North Star is not based on the truth of life energy, all of us suffer. We lose touch with our inherent personal and collective birthright.

Then came Beatrice. Beatrice was our nanny after the divorce. My mother needed someone to be home to clean, do laundry, cook, and watch over us as she was gone most of the time, including on-call overnights for her residency. Beatrice spent the nights at our house many times a week. She and her family had just relocated from Kentucky. She lived with her husband and a few of her adult children (sometimes as many as eight) in half of a double home in the inner city of Columbus, Ohio. Beatrice was small and mighty, another woman of deep faith. I loved spending time with her; I often did. I would miss school as often as I could, sometimes faking illness, just to be with Beatrice. When the two of us were alone, the house was peaceful. Where trauma made things difficult—concentrating in school or pretending that I was okay—being with Beatrice was restorative. And easy. The simplest things were so sustenance-giving. We'd go down to the basement for her to iron, and she'd break out dancing and praising Jesus, sometimes speaking in tongues. The Holy Spirit filled her! It was infectious. I learned that she was illiterate, and as our bond grew, she'd ask me to read to her and help her write. My oldest brothers sometimes fought physically in a terrifying way. Beatrice would gently touch their shoulders and say, "Jesus said it is time to stop." And they would. I was always surprised.

After my mother completed her residency, Beatrice no longer spent the nights with us. Sometimes she'd call my mother, asking if she could come to our house when her husband was drunk and threatening her. Then she would spend the night. It was around this time that she asked if I would like to come home with her. I got permission from my mother, and her daughter Anna would pick us up. I had never left our protected, elite neighborhood.

I remember the first time we drove to Beatrice's house. I was twelve years old. Beatrice and her family lived in an urban area of Columbus, a part of the city I'd never seen before. As we approached, I noticed there weren't grocery stores, but corner markets. The houses were close together. That's when I realized that my neighborhood and Beatrice's neighborhood were different.

I had more questions than I could voice. Mostly, I wondered why Beatrice, one of the best human beings I knew, was so limited in her living options. This was my first exposure to the realities of racial and economic inequities.

At that age, I didn't have cognitive understanding. I didn't know about redlining or food deserts. All I knew was that my inner knowing of the power of life in all of us did not sync with Beatrice's reality.

I've always wondered if she brought me there for her own reasons. Her husband didn't come after her when I was there. Beatrice was a safety resource for me; maybe I was for her as well.

When I was sixteen, I began volunteering at a thrift store in Beatrice's neighborhood. I was often the only white person in the store. I always felt safe, even though people thought I was crazy. I started to get mad about people thinking I should feel afraid. Through my mother and television, I'd become aware of the Civil Rights Movement. Though we didn't study it in school, I knew about Dr. Martin Luther King, Jr. and his vision. (Many years ago, I found a paper I wrote when I was twelve—at the height of the Civil Rights Movement—about Dr. King. There was one corrective comment about my grammar, but not one mention of my topic.) And yet what was burning in my heart was not reflected to me at school or in my community. Race was absent from those conversations, so I started to learn to hide my concerns about racial inequity.

It was an immense amount of effort for me to deny and distance myself from my deepest knowledge and truth. I am only including a few life experiences here to demonstrate the chasm between the true nature of life and social systems that aren't based on the source of life in everyone and everything. Our social systems don't reflect life's true nature.

In ways small and large, to conform and belong, I distanced myself from my deepest knowing. What a loss to myself and to those around me. I needed to find a way to be restored to my inner knowing, the knowing that I'd once found through my heroines.

CHAPTER 16

THE JOURNEY OF AWAKENING

In my late twenties, I landed back in Columbus, Ohio. Immediately, I became an entrepreneur, starting my business, Personal Transformation. I used Polarity principles and practices, along with other skills and tools I'd acquired, to support people aligning with their deepest and truest selves. People shared their histories and stories with me as they cultivated ways to live with purpose and clarity and offer meaningful contributions to make the world a better place. I produced trust with my clients, and through word of mouth, my business grew naturally and quickly.

During this time, more and more people shared their histories of sexual abuse with me. Back then, I had no idea how pervasive sexual abuse was.[1] The more people shared, the more my interest was piqued in exploring practices and methodologies for healing

---

1   Now, I do. Studies by David Finkelhor, Director of the Crimes Against Children Research Center, show that:
    - 1 in 5 girls and 1 in 20 boys is a victim of child sexual abuse.
    - Self-report studies show that 20% of adult females and 5-10% of adult males recall a childhood sexual assault or sexual abuse incident.

trauma. I joined a peer supervision group with clinicians where we discussed protocols to address trauma. At the same time, we were on our own doing research, comparing notes, and sharing case studies. These clinicians provided a clinical approach to use with my clients that was beyond the scope of my work. In the process of discovery, we all agreed it was necessary to know safety within oneself first in order to heal from trauma. Without inner safety, trauma holds trauma, and there is no resource for recovery.

Polarity was a perfect fit to help support people finding their inner safety. From my own healing through Polarity, I found a way to rest in the pulsing radiance inside of me. I also knew my heroines Grace, Mercy, and Love. Knowing my inner safety gave me hope and a pathway for healing. I knew I could help people find their inner safety with their own life energy. My office partner for many years, Janice George, LISW, and I shared many clients. We realized our collective skills made a powerful impact on our clients who'd suffered sexual abuse, and eventually we created a training for sexual abuse conferences to support healing of sexual trauma from a clinical and energetic perspective.

In a small way, we were supporting people healing from a systemic issue of sexual violence. This was rewarding. I was acting based on my inner knowing and activating my internal power—while addressing a social issue.

Along the way, one of my clients invited me to contribute my expertise around Polarity and the energy components of healing trauma to The Ohio AIDS Coalition's healing weekends. I'd been socialized to be afraid of people with HIV and AIDS. I'd seen people be judged and ostracized. However, I trusted this individual. Whatever heedless fears I had disappeared on that first healing weekend. My world continued to expand. Through my involvement with the AIDS community, I learned about health care disparities through a racial, class, and gender lens.

As I took off the blinders, my humanitarian nature flourished. Suddenly I found myself feeling compassion for people from all walks of life, people who were experiencing challenges and circumstances far beyond my own understanding. My caring knew no bounds. I was fundamentally changed.

Soon after my work with the Ohio AIDS Coalition, an entrepreneur client asked me to provide team building for his team. I admitted that was outside my scope of training. He insisted. While discovering his desired outcomes, I designed a training born out of my understanding of Polarity principles and how interconnected systems could work. I found a way to translate the language to a business model. I explained that it would be an experiment. It was successful. I found I loved working with individuals and teams, helping them unite around a shared team mission to serve their organization.

I had outgrown Personal Transformation. What I wanted to offer was something different, something that could serve businesses and organizations as well as individuals. That's what inspired me to start my next business, UnifyingSolutions. Centered on generating sustainable change through coaching and consulting, UnifyingSolutions is a perfect business name for me. It incorporates the essence of Polarity. After all, unity is at the center of the poles. Unity is where dynamic aliveness lives. Solutions provide pathways to greater aliveness through unity.

I realized I needed professional development to support my instinctual knowledge. I wanted to gain skills and techniques, while growing professionally and personally. I attended Strozzi Institute's Embodied Leadership Pathway. I completed my Master Coaching Certification with them, and for a brief period of time was a faculty member. During my Master training, two key factors altered my purpose: my awakening and my reunion with my deeper knowing.

Going into the Master coaching program, I thought my project would be on Timely-Relevant Feedback. I believed doing so would put me on the map professionally as an expert. However, while answering their meaningful questions to determine what our project would be, we were asked what we wanted our legacy to be through impact in the world. I discovered it was not Timely-Relevant Feedback. What came alive for me instead was awakening leadership in women in order to increase representation and generate-positive change in the world. Mind you, I was two years into doing qualitative research with leaders from Wall Street, CEOs of for-profit and non-profit companies, managers at Trader Joe's—you name it. I'd started writing the first chapter of a book on the subject, and all of a sudden, I found myself at a fork in the road: Would I follow my deeper calling and shift directions? Or would I continue on with Timely-Relevant Feedback, which I thought would make me successful in the business world?

I took a pause. Breathed, meditated, sat with myself. I realized I could still use the material from Timely-Relevant Feedback to create trainings for teams and organizations, which I have done many times since. I abandoned the book and the unrealized potential of ego glorification.

Instead, I took a chance on what was calling me from within—the deeper than that. I'm so glad I did. I created a public course, Women Generating: Collective Power for Positive Change. How could I predict how this would start me on the journey of returning to my own inner knowing?

The next major factor that occurred during my Master Coaching Training was through one of my instructors, Staci Haines. Staci introduced me to the concept of intersectionality, as developed by Kimberlé Crenshaw. The Oxford Dictionary defines intersectionality as "the interconnected nature of social categorizations such as race, class, and gender, regarded as creating overlapping and interdependent systems of discrimination or disadvantage." From Staci I learned how social norms and historical forces have the power to shape our thoughts, feelings, and embodiment at an unconscious level.

This was a new paradigm for me. As I learned, I embedded these concepts into the formation and development of Women Generating. There was an interweaving of growing understanding, both internally and externally, that unfolded over the years and continues to unfold. Remember: Life is kindergarten from birth to death. This was kindergarten again. Seeds were planted that kept germinating on my evolving journey.

During the training at Strozzi Institute, we were required to do our own assessment of how these social systems of dominance and oppression lived inside of us. I'd never considered that level of shaping in myself. Suddenly I had to pause, get curious, and willingly be uncomfortable in order to know my true self better. The intersecting systems of oppression utilized for this undertaking were economic supremacy (class), white supremacy (I know that term is hard for many people—I will help you find it liberating), Christian supremacy (differentiated from faith), and male supremacy. We were asked to examine how these forces became engrained in institutions and communities and how they eventually trickled down to our families and intimate networks. If you've ever been in therapy, perhaps you've done self-examination in direct relationship to your family. This was a very different approach. I had to examine how social norms and historical forces filtered down to shape my family, and therefore, me.

This became crucial for me on my quest to return to my deepest knowing. Polarity is the restoration of the mind to neutrality. Certainly, my mind had inherited false narratives about who does and doesn't have value. These narratives date back to the height of colonization. How were these unconscious, hidden beliefs keeping me from my deepest self? I wanted to excavate what was in my mind to build a true narrative of equity, a narrative of dignity for all and universal access to resources. I had a ways to go to restore my mind. I was both scared and excited. I didn't know what I would uncover, yet I believed it would bring me to greater resonance with my inner knowing, which had been there all along. This was an education I never received in school.

Following my deeper passion to invent a course like Women Generating while addressing systems of dominance and oppression, I was guided to my greater potential. Suddenly I was tapping into creativity, purpose, liberation, and vibrancy in ways I could never have imagined. I continued to be guided by this undertaking, and along the way, my life began to restructure and evolve. Following life energy and its ask of me became a vital gift that has led me to this book and to you!

CHAPTER 17

THE INTERWEAVING
EVOLUTION

Women Generating incorporated embodied, somatic practices into its training modules. This was a unique approach to leadership in general—and especially for women leaders. I created an open-ended intake form upon registration for the class to determine what women were seeking for themselves. Universally, women reported wanting to increase their confidence. But there was more crossover. CEOs, entry-level employees, stay-at-home moms: These women all faced similar challenges. They battled perfectionism, the need to be the perfect employee . . . *and* the perfect partner . . . *and* the perfect mother. They suffered from imposter syndrome, doubting their own value in the workplace, worrying they weren't worthy of their seat at the proverbial table. And they lacked support, all while engaging in pro bono emotional labor, tending to those around them. Why were these themes so prevalent? I became curious and wondered what they might have to do with systems of oppression.

I began to see these themes as collective challenges, even though they're experienced at a very personal level. I decided to design practices to address these challenges in order to shift both the embodiment and narrative for these women. I wanted them to trust their power, trust their inner knowing, build systems of support, and unify the women in a generative community of support.

I enrolled Julie Graber, an expert on data for women's leadership, to partner in doing qualitative research with two interns from The Ohio State University. We followed the women throughout the six-week course, and they were interviewed every month for the following six months.

From research, Julie and I knew that girls' confidence peaks around nine years old, declining from ages ten to fourteen. ROX (Ruling Our eXperiences) has detailed nationwide research that shares the challenges girls face. Confidence Code for Girls is another great resource. An organization I support is Black Girl Rising Inc.: Keeping Black Girls at Promise.

Women leaders were reporting how these social norms impacted their sense of self in their leadership. Almost every woman I've coached has in her own way spoken about imposter syndrome.

Girls in their teen years are taught to be driven by image instead of internal value and worth. They're brought into comparison and competition. These habits persisted in women leaders. Women compete against one another because we haven't had the same historical longevity of sports teams and military service to learn to fight, win, and/or survive together. Julie and I became more committed to ensuring that women gained access to their power, regained trust in their inner value and worth, and practiced supporting one another.

One of the practices I designed was concentric circles. The women would join in pairs—one partner joining the outer circle to signify standing behind and thus "being a stand for" the women who made up the inner circle. Each woman had a partner behind her (with consent and determination of distance). The woman on the inner circle would turn and face her partner, sharing what she stood for. For instance, she might say, "I stand for my dignity and the dignity of all beings." Then she'd turn back around. The woman in the outer circle would stand with grounded presence, arms extended with palms open toward her partner. She'd repeat, "I stand with and for you, honoring your dignity and the dignity of all beings." The woman in the inner circle received and experienced what it was like to have another woman stand with and for her, for what she truly cared about. The practice often brought tears of gratitude, relief, and joy as well as a sense of shared power. This interrupted the social norms among women of enduring, over-exerting, proving, feeling under-supported, and experiencing isolation.

Another practice I designed, collective power, unified women to shift from competition and comparison to generative power. In that practice, the women stood together in a circle. Each woman shared what they stood for that no one could take away from them. They declared their value. I decided to interweave my understanding of Polarity into this practice. I knew that life energy is in everyone and everything. In Polarity, the element of ether is the essence of life energy. Ether is in everyone and everything sent through the source for all of creation. Ether connects us to the source. The joints represent ether in the body. I wondered if we made contact at the wrists, if the currency of life would run through our collective unit, uniting us through the gift of life. I decided to experiment. I introduced it into the training to see what would happen. People were reluctant at first. I am not a touchy-feely person, and as a sexual abuse survivor I always want consent in touch. I wanted to go slow and be deliberate, to support everyone understanding the purpose of the experiment. While people were willing, it was awkward at first. However, the longer we stood there, the more the energy started pulsing. It was undeniable. People became uplifted; they reported feeling connected, empowered, and grounded. There was a sense of ease. We were in the process of building a social system of women becoming generative and connected and sharing their power. This was contrary to the social shaping women reported in their intake forms.

This was a game changer.

Julie and I saw women change over time; those women brought the changes into their organizations and businesses. Women Generating evolved into Women Generating: Collective Power for Positive Change.

INTERSECTION OF RACE AND GENDER

While I was developing Women Generating, I was also unpacking my own internalization of systems of dominance and oppression. As I started researching the oppression of white supremacy, I realized I had a steep learning curve. Yes, I had sensitivity to the harm of racism, and I had exposure. However, I hadn't looked at what it really meant for me to be white. Nor had I really looked at white supremacy. The term white supremacy can be very alienating or off-putting. At that time, I found it both threatening and potentially liberating. Staci had seen in me a passion for racial equity more than I even saw in myself. She suggested I start reading books to help me on my journey. I was arrogant and didn't think I needed to read. I believed that caring and being a good person was enough. Soon enough, that notion was challenged when I had missteps with people I cared about. Being a good person was and is not enough.

I wanted to know what I didn't know so that I could reduce harm as much as possible.

I began reading about the history of colonization, the slave trade, racism, and white privilege. I read historical fiction. I watched documentaries and movies, followed activists on Instagram. I listened to podcasts. The more I learned, the more I wanted to learn. My blinders started coming off, and I began to realize that my mind had gotten corrupted with lies. Until I became conscious of how my mind had absorbed the inaccuracy of history, I would be limited and potentially produce harm. I'm not talking about Ku Klux Klan harm. I'm talking about dismissing a Black person's voice. Discrediting their idea. Maybe even demonizing a Black person. Good person or not, I had the potential to do so.

Once I started to observe my mind, I saw evidence of the corruption that had been unbeknownst to me prior.

Recall the three aspects of the mind in the You section of the book: the super-conscious mind, the conscious mind, and the unconscious mind. When the unconscious mind is inundated with unconscious material, it weighs down the parasympathetic function to support nourishment, repair, and sustenance for our physical body. The conscious mind, which is designed to be neutral, is programmed with bias, judgements, and limited perspective. The soul, trying to inform and inspire the mind, is unable to do its job. This applies to social systems' unconscious control of me, you, and everyone.

I was socialized to be racist. Until I could make myself conscious of that fact, even if my heart and mind told me I wasn't, I could be hurtful.

The pervasiveness of my own biases and judgments showed up in the most mundane circumstances. One day I was talking with a Black woman as we were creating an agenda for an upcoming training. In my head, I heard myself thinking, "Wow, you are so smart for a Black woman!" My own thought process stunned me. Where had it come from? Thank goodness I hadn't said it out loud, but still. I'd thought it. I don't qualify a white woman's intelligence. Experiencing this made me watch my mind more closely. If that could arise, what else?

At the time, my husband and I lived in a liberal white neighborhood. A Black friend was staying with us for a while. Over the years, she'd house- and dog-sat for us. One day a neighbor saw our friend and called the police for suspicious behavior. We decided it was time to move. We relocated to an urban environment. I was unfamiliar with men walking by with low hanging pants and hooded sweatshirts. I started to flinch, and I thought to myself, "Where is this flinching coming from?" I had no reason to flinch. I questioned myself to determine if there was truly any danger, and the answer was no. I had to decondition myself from being socialized to see hoodies on Black men as dangerous.

Another way racism shows up in me is around what I call white threat. Over the years, I have had the good fortune to facilitate trainings with Black women and men. When their expertise starts to shine, and the feedback given to them is positive, I can feel my hackles go up *even while I am happy for them*. I know the signal and feeling associated with the threat, so I interrupt it. I sense my body leaning forward; I want to repeat what they just said. These are signs of me protecting my superiority. I say to myself, "Give it up, Suzanne." I laugh at myself. I don't want to act any of that out. I hold my mind accountable. I keep a race and other isms lens in my mind as much as possible. I believe we all need to keep these lenses in our minds if we want to see the true value and dignity in every human being. Otherwise, the way we are socialized will win in spite of our good hearts.

One of the ways I came to understand internalized racism was through the Three-Fifths Compromise dating back to 1787. The compromise was developed in reference to including slaves into a state's population. For the purpose of legislative and taxation reasons, three out of every five slaves were counted. The mentality that Black people have three-fifths value wasn't explicitly stated, yet it was implicitly affirmed. I saw reflections of the dehumanization represented in every aspect of civil engagement. While the Three-Fifths Compromise was eventually abolished in 1868, Black people in this country were not awarded true humanity. My friend and colleague Maurice Stevens brought it to my attention—*what does it mean to have the two-fifths more?* I was riveted. *What did it mean to be white?*

I learned that whiteness developed as a race as a social construct in the seventeenth century. The purpose of it was to justify land displacement, genocide, and slavery. Irish and Italian immigrants experienced horrific conditions in our country prior to becoming seen as white. Sister Cabrini found the living conditions inhumane for Italian immigrants. With the advance of the slave trade, Italians and Irish climbed one rung up over slaves; they became white.

Inherent in being white, I discovered, is an unearned superiority, that two-fifths more. I began to see how I needed to protect my advantage and comfort without ever realizing it before. As I sat with all of this, I began to thaw at a deeper level inside of myself. I didn't realize how distant I had become to my deepest self. This was, and is, an uncomfortable awakening. Labor for birth is painful and challenging, requiring work. This labor is also painful—and also so life-giving. My whole being began to align around life-giving principles.

Back at Women Generating, I wanted my classes to diversify. At this point, people in the community had exposure to my journey. At networking events, when I met new people, I shared my story. I began talking openly about race. I spoke with my clients about systems of oppression. As my network grew, I began fostering relationships with people who didn't look like me. I was there to earn trust—not to presume I deserved trust as a white person. By having open conversations with everyone, people slowly did begin to trust me. One Black woman leader was interested in the Women Generating six-part series. After the first two classes, she asked if she could give me feedback. She shared that she loved the training, the embodied practices, the homework in-between. What she did not appreciate was being the only Black woman in the room. As a senior leader, she faced that all day long. After hours, she wanted to train in a room where there were other people who looked like her, both in the class and on the teaching team. I'm so grateful she gave me this feedback. I took a hard look at the cost to her being in the workforce; I thought about the micro- and macro-aggressions she must experience every day. I'd overlooked that reality. I also had to ask myself if I was tokenizing her. How serious was I about change?

I decided I would build more relationships until I had at least three women of color in the class. I also let them know if they loved the work, I wanted to build facilitators so there would be representation on the leadership team.

Word got out to a broader community. The conversation in Women Generating became truly intersectional, including all women. Race was talked about openly as well as other factors of oppression. Soon enough the pathway to the teaching team was fifty percent racially diverse.

Around this time, James A. White, Sr.[2] and I became acquaintances. On our first meeting, we sat and talked about race and racism for two hours. We kept meeting every few weeks. Jim welcomed the opportunity to ask me, a white woman, questions he did not feel comfortable asking other people. I listened to his life experiences; I shared mine; we talked about history, books, and built a bond through our conversations.

One day, I asked Jim, "If people could listen to us talk openly, humanize across our differences, be uncomfortable and safe, challenge ourselves and each other, do you think more people would have a living example of what is possible? If we aren't able to have conversations about race, what chance is there to find solutions for systemic racism?" Jim agreed these were good questions. Columbus, Ohio, where I lived at the time, ranked 55th for economic and racial segregation in the country. The possibility of randomly having coffee and these types of conversations was highly unlikely.

At the same time, I was also developing a trusted relationship with Dr. Sierra Austin, who then worked at the YWCA. Together, we approached the Y to offer a course called Safe Conversation About Race. Sierra would moderate, and Jim and I would dialogue. Our first session was held during a wicked blizzard with frigid temperatures. We thought we might have twenty or thirty people at most. No—150 people showed up. 150. The room was

---

2   Meet James: https://www.youtube.com/watch?v=r9DDE7NV1Nw

SUZANNE ROBERTS | 135

almost fifty percent racially diverse. We had to keep bringing in chairs to accommodate everyone. For the next three years, we continued to offer the event quarterly in tandem with The Columbus Foundation. We never had crowds of less than 150. We brought people into conversation with one another after our portion, and we witnessed conversations across racial differences, where humanizing one another was occurring.

At these events, Jim and I started with history, dating back to a barter system of shared resources, to the advance of currency, from colonization through Europe to our own history here in the United States. Both Sierra and Jim have extensive knowledge and ways to elucidate history and bring everyone up to speed.

I began to see race at the bottom of every intersection of oppression. I care about all marginalized communities. As Erin Upchurch, Executive Director of Kaleidoscope, a Columbus-based organization supporting LGBTQIA+ youth in Ohio, puts it, "Race is the prism through which all difference is cast."

I examined the statement that "we are all one" through the lens of Polarity. If the positive pole is truly the soul influencing and the material world is the negative pole—the mind neutral, yes—then the reflection of life in everyone and everything would be evident on this plane. But because social systems of dominance and oppression have their own momentum, our material world predominantly reflects these systems. The reality of us all being one becomes theoretical. The only way for that to be possible would be for the majority of human beings on this planet to make our minds join in neutrality. Then our social systems would be guided by soul qualities collectively. Every life would be valued and reflected in all aspects of civic engagement. There would be equal access and equal opportunities. However, that's not the case.

The hallmark of my trainings incorporated collective power, just as it had in Women Generating. Humanizing across differences without sanitizing oppression is the standard for everything I do and become. In this way, I am honoring that life is indeed in everyone and everything, while oppression is occurring on the material plane. While I can't control the world and stop racism, sexism, and all the isms, I can stay awake and generate positive change while reducing harm. That matters to me deeply. I want to be a true representative of life.

I had no idea what I was walking into through choosing Women Generating and tackling systems of dominance and oppression. The journey kept bringing me closer and closer to my inner knowing, guiding me to act on behalf of that knowing and to truly value the life in everyone and everything.

CHAPTER 18

THE RECONFIGURATION AND RESTORATION

I could no longer teach Polarity or run my business through an individualistic lens. I needed to teach and coach through the lens of interconnectedness with the interweb of life. My awareness of intersectionality, systems of dominance, and oppression required me to build leaders and design social fabric to reflect the true nature of life energy while acknowledging the impacts of dominance and oppression on all of us.

Women Generating reflected a shift in my consciousness. I built racially diverse teaching teams. I was ready to hand over the half-day trainings. Anne Santilli, my long-time friend and colleague, agreed to mentor the teaching pods. She'd studied Polarity with me for ten years prior to my teaching sabbatical. After observing the facilitation teams, she came to the conclusion that there was a gap in their capacity to be successful in the trainings. She believed the only way they would develop their capacity would be through Polarity. I was on my eight-year sabbatical from teaching. Anne looked me straight in the eyes and said, "It's time to teach again." She knew the way I teach Polarity would be essential for the teaching team to develop greater presence, more neutrality, and the ability to hold space for the people in the room.

I agreed.

Individual and collective transformation and liberation had become inseparable for me, therefore my new iteration of Polarity became "Polarity for Human and Social Development."

My unwavering focus on teaching Polarity is on one thing and one thing only: Our soul consciousness, pulsing at the center of our being, is awaiting our homecoming. This is our birthright. Life is to be found inside of us through connecting with our vital soul current. Seeking within is our only true fulfillment. Soul consciousness is operating through form as our inherent design to know the truth of who we are consciously—a radiant being. Our life energy is connected to the source, our center point of focus, providing our life with a direction and purpose.

As I always have throughout my polarity teaching, I remained laser focused on soul consciousness operating through form to consciously remember itself. We do so by turning our attention inward, remembering and returning to our inner treasure over and over again. Turning your attention inward to seek the treasure of your own soul requires focused presence. The choice to remember and return to your inner treasure over and over again requires dedication. Stillness at the center of your being is where your treasure is found. It takes time to build capacity to stay with stillness. It's not always easy to keep in mind that the path of Polarity is "kindergarten for life" or that the practice of seeking within requires dedication and commitment for the long haul.

As my teaching continued to evolve, I incorporated the collective power practice into my curriculum. The collective power practice is based on Polarity intelligence—essentially, the knowledge that life energy is in everyone and everything. Through the design of this practice, soul currency at the center of one's being awakens and is amplified.

Ether, the only neutral element, is the link between our deepest self and the source of life for all of creation. Ether represents the longing of our own soul to return home to itself, our own homecoming. Ether is our soul consciousness, freedom, stillness, and conscious choice. Ether is the pulsing energy of our soul in our cerebral spinal fluid. The more still our mind is, the more potent the power of the ether current is at the center of our being, the more vibrant we are in a restful state. Ether is the essence of energy in all forms of life and links us through this neutral, life-giving energy to all of creation. I developed the collective power practice based on this intelligence. We are meant to be conscious of and connected to the interweb of life.

The joints in our body reflect the element of ether. To mimic a biodiverse forest, we come together as a group in a circle, in all of our glorious diversity. Drawing inspiration from the intelligence of trees, we imagine belonging to a complex, intertwined, root system with all of our unique energy currents creating a powerful infrastructure. In a forest, the strongest roots support the weakest roots. We apply this analogy to inform our social group, becoming more alive and interconnected, providing care for the whole of the group. Our collective thriving becomes our essential and natural blueprint for our human social system. Our social fabric gets designed with the necessity of the vibrancy of each unique human, each person cherished, connected, and valued. All are included in the vital health of the living system.

With this knowledge, we then connect at the wrists, not from personality to personality, rather from the essence of life to the essence of life within each other, with ether as our point of connection. What happens next is astounding. Slowly the etheric current starts building vibrant power. Throughout the living collective system, support starts feeding the whole from the infrastructure of our shared roots. People start to experience rest and access to deep resource as they deepen in connection. As people start resting, they begin to discover that in that rest, their sense of safety and belonging is within them. Rooting in Collective Power awakens inner safety, belonging, value, and aliveness. Now diversity and inclusion are experienced as living realities, not just good ideas. Together we become who we truly are, *alive*, in unity, as a diverse human living system. We acknowledge the harm of systems of dominance and oppression. We unite with living energy at our shared center without sanitizing oppression.

This is often the first time people have experienced their own inner radiance while experiencing rest and support. For marginalized people who have historically been undervalued, the experience of truly being included is novel. Vibrancy is now accessible underneath any internalized oppression. This new paradigm is liberating. With newly experienced freedom along with an understanding of the power of the true nature of interconnectedness, a growing awareness arises of embodying social change. Social systems that devalue and marginalize have negative impacts on inner power and radiance. Our unconscious awareness often colludes with these social systems, and we end up diminishing the true power of ourselves. Owning and embodying radiant power disproves that narrative. Outer forces no longer determine unapologetic radiance. Unapologetic radiance becomes the new norm.

With this growing awareness, it became clear to me that I would require my teaching team and the participants to be fifty percent racially diverse. I wanted the opportunity to build personal and collective liberation that reflects the truth of life energy. I know that forests thrive best in biodiversity. I wanted to ensure my rooms were filled with complex diversity in terms of age, race, gender identification, class, and religion. They are. I've witnessed over and over again every person in the room enlivened through collective power, truly included, genuinely required to radiate their full unapologetic power for the sake of the whole living system. The joy, the gratitude, the connection, the ground, and the living vitality of the whole is hard to find words for. I only wish everyone had the opportunity to experience the vibrancy of diversity uniting around life energy within all of us without sanitizing oppression.

During this time, I also had the good fortune of providing a monthly Leadership and Polarity program with Michele Morin for five years at Marion Correctional Institute in their reintegration unit. We did collective power monthly. To see incarcerated men expanding in their dignity, connecting life to life, and truly belonging is also beyond words.

Some of my Polarity students have brought me into their teams. They wanted their team to experience collective power. At first, I was hesitant. I had kept my Polarity knowledge separate from my coaching and consulting business, UnifyingSolutions, but I took the risk at their encouragement to build collective power with their leadership team. Once again, I witnessed the impact of this practice and the sense of aliveness, shared power, and unity that it induces. Once again, the power of unity of life reveals itself over and over again.

COLLECTIVE POWER

Collective power builds social fabric based on life principles.

In the balance between two poles, there is always a center point. We connect with *life* at the center point of building our social fabric. We live by the true nature of life: The source sends life to everyone and everything. The living system then cares and nourishes the whole with innate intelligence, like a forest. The health of the living collective community calls for each and every person to be as fully vibrant as possible. We become a collective living system of liberation.

Our truth of belonging, connection, value, dignity, and safety is found through tuning in to the currency of life flowing inside of us. Life never leaves us. We all belong to life. We all are truly safe in life. Life is our value, our dignity, our worth. We've already been given it; we don't earn it—we get to learn it by becoming our wholeness and holiness. It already resides inside of us.

Polarity is a pathway for me, you, and everyone. Polarity guides us to our vibrancy, purpose, and liberation.

At the end of the day, *I am, We are.*

Thank you for joining me on the journey of *It's Deeper Than That* for The Great Reconnection™ to your soul.

I am safe inside my inner stillness

I belong to the radiant life within me

I act on behalf of my vital life force

I am grateful for my self and the gift of my life

I am one with the river of life, we are

BIBLIOGRAPHY

Berkeley. "Most to Least Targeted Cities." Accessed May 22, 2025. https://belonging.berkeley.edu/most-least-segregated-cities.

Collins. "Bias." Accessed December 12, 2024. https://www.collinsdictionary.com/us/dictionary/english/bias.

Eberhardt, Jennifer L. *Biased: Uncovering the Hidden Prejudice That Shapes What We See, Think, and Do.* Penguin Books, 2019.

Etymonline. "Origin and History of Discernment." Accessed January 7, 2025. https://www.etymonline.com/word/discernment.

Finkelhor, David, Anne Shattuck, Heather A. Turner, and Sherry L. Hamby. "The Lifetime Prevalence of Child Sexual Abuse and Sexual Assault Assessed in Late Adolescence."

Journal of Adolescent Health 55, no. 3 (September 2014): 329–33. https://doi.org/10.1016/j.jadohealth.2013.12.026.

NAACP. "Criminal Justice Fact Sheet." Accessed May 20, 2025. https://naacp.org/resources/criminal-justice-fact-sheet.

Neurolaunch editorial team. "Behavioral Confirmation: How Expectations Shape Social Interactions." *Neurolaunch*, September 22, 2024. https://neurolaunch.com/behavioral-confirmation/.

Stone, Randolph. *Health Building: The Conscious Art of Living Well.* Book Publishing Company, 1999.

- -. *Polarity Therapy: The Complete Collected Works on This Revolutionary Healing Art by the Originator of the System, Vol. One.* Book Publishing Company, 1999.

- -. *Polarity Therapy: The Complete Collected Works on This Revolutionary Healing Art by the Originator of the System, Vol. Two.* Book Publishing Company, 1999.

Tierney, Abigail. "Female to Male Earnings Ratio of Workers in the U.S. in 2023, By State." *Statista*, October 28, 2024 https://www.statista.com/statistics/244361/female-to-male-earnings-ratio-of-workers-in-the-us-by-state/.

Tierney, Abigail. "U.S. Median Household Income 2023, by Race and Ethnicity." *Statista*, September 16, 2024. https://www.statista.com/statistics/233324/median-household-income-in-the-united-states-by-race-or-ethnic-group/.

"What Is Implicit Bias?" *Psychology Today*, October 13, 2019. https://www.psychologytoday.com/us/blog/spontaneous-thoughts/201910/what-is-implicit-bias.

ACKNOWLEDGEMENTS

I'm grateful beyond words for all the support I received to help make this book possible. I knew I had a book in me, yet I was reluctant to write, as writing, until now, was not something I was deeply practiced at. My Polarity students begged me to write a book, to make Polarity more accessible and easier to read.

Two writing coaches, Sara Connell and Alexis Wilson, believed in what I had to say from the beginning. Alexis started me on my path of writing. Thank you, Alexis, for your creativity and wisdom that helped me start pouring out what was inside of me. Sara, you inspire me to reach for my biggest dreams and to make my greatest possible impact. Through Sara's organization, Thought Leader Academy, I connected with my mentor, Amy Fortney. Amy, your trust in me and your thoughtful, meaningful support has carried me through challenges and triumphs.

My Polarity Therapy teachers shaped and guided me to become the human being I am today. Jim Feil, thank you for "It's Deeper Than That" in my very first class. Thank you for reading this book and providing your testimony.

Cindy Brown Rawlinson, you are not here for me to thank. I know I did while you were alive. We tried to write a book together about Polarity—our work informed this book. I hope I'm making you proud. Ray Castellino is no longer here either. He provided me an opportunity to teach Polarity yoga in his office after I completed my training, and his work lives on in me today.

My embodiment sisters: Mandy Blake, Renee Gregorio, Robyn McCulloch, Chris Johnson, and Beth Davis. Thank you for creating a safe and supportive sisterhood for my transformation and empowerment and for trailblazing the path for me to write this book. Robyn, Women Generating would not be here without your unconventional coaching and guidance. The walks along the paths and rim of the Rio Grande River in New Mexico, you asking me to notice what grabbed my attention, became the bedrock of the vision for Women Generating. Mandy, our recent connection has brought me to greater depths of compassion around love and loss. Being by your side means the world to me.

Richard Strozzi-Heckler and Staci Haines provided leadership and guidance at Strozzi Institute. Staci, thank you for introducing me to intersectionality, intersecting systems of oppression, and calling me to do my deeper work around race and other isms to become the person I am today.

A few years ago, I brought four years of writing about Polarity and my life in an unedited, disorganized package to Louise Robertson as a writing coach. The stack of printed material was two to three inches high. Louise, your editorial prowess and honesty allowed me to release that old material and conceive the book anew.

As it became clear that I needed to start over, I had no idea what the shape of the book should look like.

My son Akiva and his grandmother and my dear friend, Laurel Richardson, guided me to the organizational structure of the book. Akiva, you taught me that readers needed to care about me first in order to care about Polarity. Laurel, as a renowned worldwide author in her field of sociology, gave me tremendous feedback and support. One day when I was reading to her, she declared, "This book has three sections—Me, You, and Everyone." A light bulb went off in my head. Thanks to Laurel, I finally had a structure for the book.

Emily Levin joined me as a writing coach as the book was emerging. Invaluable in helping me tighten sentences to create greater impact, Emily also encouraged me to trust my voice. Monu Singh gave innumerable hours of support for the book. Dana Brown, you are truly a beta reader extraordinaire.

Dwylette Montgomery chose the color blue for the drop representing the soul. Dwylette, your friendship and ongoing support have made all of the work about Polarity come to life.

Two therapists played a major role in my healing and transformation: Dr. Mark Elliott and Dr. Tanisha Knighton. You both prepared me for greater visibility for the launch of the book and the documentary.

When I joined Sara Connell's Thought Leadership Academy, I was assigned a writing coach, JoAnna Novak. Through her editing and feedback, I learned how to listen to what I was writing and bring intentionality to my voice. JoAnna, you are in every page of this book with me.

Anne Santilli, I've known you for thirty-two years. You have been a student of Polarity since I first began teaching. Your kindness and care for life is rare. Your pessimism meets my optimism, and we land in the middle, both of us better because of each other. Your friendship is sustenance to my life.

My Polarity Teaching Team. Sharonda Crome, your soulful wisdom and inner knowing enriches the team and participants. Arnesia McMillan, your inner attunement and vitality are infectious. Maurice Stevens, Jelise Guynn, Jennifer Adams, Rachel

Woods, and Erin Upchurch, you each bring depth and support every time you join our teaching team.

Jelise Guynn and Juli Rogers provided the beautiful graphics for the book.

Karen Hewitt and Dr. Sierra Austin, I love walking alongside you with Polarity as a liberatory practice.

James A. White, Sr., Dr. Sierra Austin, Melony Brunson, and L.C. Johnson partnered with me to have collective impact through Safe Conversation About Race (Healing the SCAR).

Patty Kimball, thirteen years as my Assistant, you make my life and world possible.

Raeden Gibran, your unique creativity, your ancient wisdom, your partnership for social media came right at the right time.

Aujie Baker, the documentary would not exist without you, your team, and your creative genius. I trust you with my life.

LaChandra and Brian Baker, your support of the documentary project is invaluable.

Qiana Williams, you stepped in without hesitation to interview me for the documentary.

Deb Cannon and family, LaWanda Thompson, and Pannsy Brown, you are in my heart.

The Laskin family is my family of choice. Jeanne, you are a sister to me. David, you taught me presence and love beyond language. Beth and Jacob, I've known you since birth. Beth, you are like a daughter to me.

Shauna and Tony Juarez, your support sustained me through writing my book, many meals, and conversations.

Betty McKee and my siblings from another mother, I'm grateful to you and your love.

Laurie Goodman and Julie Harmon, my friends since pre-school. A lifetime of friendship is rare. I'm lucky to know you and have you in my life.

Paula Levin, Rabbi Josh Brown, Torah Study, you all have enriched my life and learning.

Sophia Laettner Joubert, friend and editor, you came into my life at just the right time. You made the manuscript into its final voice.

Jennifer Walton at Sky Nile Consulting for PR for the documentary and book premiere.

Jehan LLC Photography for capturing me.

My husband, Glen Kizer, and I reconnected after 38 years and married. Glen, you mean the world to me. You are my true friend and companion for life. Your patience, kindness, and gentle spirit are an inspiration to me to become a better person every day. You have been an integral part of every stage of this book.

Adam, Yewyn, and Akiva, my three sons. I'm grateful to each of you and am in awe of who you have become as adults. You are kind, sensitive men. Adam, thank you for being a living example for me as a composer, keeping pen to paper until a piece of complex music becomes complete. Yewyn, thank you for your love of the natural world, your sensitivity and healing presence, and your delicious food. Akiva, thank you for your guidance on this book, for your honesty, and for being your unapologetic self. I love you all so much and am grateful to be your mother.

I have been with my twin grandchildren, Sasha and Aiden, since birth. I am honored to be your Gaga. You bring me great joy. I love you to the farthest galaxy and back.

Ava and Lyla Woerth, Cecilia, and Phoebe Kizer, I love being in your lives. You all are amazing, creative, kind human beings.

Vicki Kolomensky, Elizabeth and Brian Woerth, Alex Kizer and Robin Ventura, Katie and Alejandro Montenegro, and Rebekah Ferriel, you all enrich my life.

I know there are more people to thank. I would need to write another book to truly thank all the people that have supported and loved me into this moment. Please know I appreciate each and every one of you.

I am aware in writing these acknowledgements how fortunate I am to be surrounded by so many people in my village and life. I am eternally grateful.

ABOUT THE AUTHOR

In *It's Deeper Than That: Pathway to a Vibrant, Purposeful, and Liberated Life*, Suzanne Roberts offers a bold invitation into remembering, reconnection, and transformation. Blending five decades of lived experience with insights from science and metaphysics, she reveals the deeper forces shaping our lives and calls us back to our deepest self—the truth of who we are.

Through UnifyingSolutions and her pioneering body of work, The Great Reconnection™, Suzanne guides individuals, teams, and communities into new ways of living and leading that restore clarity, vibrancy, and purpose.

As a coach, author, facilitator, and speaker, Suzanne has dedicated her life to transformation that touches both individuals and society at large.

Based in Akron, Ohio, she finds renewal in nature, often hiking and kayaking in the beauty of Northeast Ohio. She shares her life with her husband and three dogs and treasures time with her family and friends.